Territory

Short Introductions to Geography are highly accessible books designed to introduce key geographical concepts to students. Taking a concise approach, these introductions convey a sense of the intellectual liveliness, differing perspectives, and key debates that have developed around each concept. The central ground is covered and readers are encouraged to think in new and critical ways about concepts that are core to geographical study. The series will serve a vital pedagogic function for students and instructors.

Published

GIS: A Short Introduction
Nadine Schuurman

Place: A Short Introduction
Tim Cresswell

Territory: A Short Introduction
David Delaney

In Preparation

Maps: A Short Introduction
Matthew Edney

Territory
a short introduction

David Delaney

Blackwell
Publishing

BLACKWELL PUBLISHING
350 Main Street, Malden, MA 02148-5020, USA
9600 Garsington Road, Oxford OX4 2DQ, UK
550 Swanston Street, Carlton, Victoria 3053, Australia

The right of David Delaney to be identified as the Author of this Work has been asserted in accordance with the UK Copyright, Designs, and Patents Act 1988.

First published 2005 by Blackwell Publishing Ltd

1 2005

Library of Congress Cataloging-in-Publication Data

Delaney, David.
    Territory : a short introduction/David Delaney.
       p. cm. – (Short introductions to geography)
    Includes bibliographical references and index.
    ISBN-13: 978-1-4051-1831-6 (hard cover : alk. paper)
    ISBN-10: 1-4051-1831-8 (hard cover : alk. paper)
    ISBN-13: 978-1-4051-1832-3 (pbk. : alk. paper)
    ISBN-10: 1-4051-1832-6 (pbk. : alk. paper)
    1. Human geography. 2. Human territoriality. I. Title. II. Series.
    GF43.D45 2005
    304.2′3–dc22
                                    2005003247

A catalogue record for this title is available from the British Library.

Set in 10/12pt Palatino
by SPI Publisher Services, Pondicherry, India
Printed and bound in India
by Replika Press, Pvt Ltd, India

The publisher's policy is to use permanent paper from mills that operate a sustainable forestry policy, and which has been manufactured from pulp processed using acid-free and elementary chlorine-free practices. Furthermore, the publisher ensures that the text paper and cover board used have met acceptable environmental accreditation standards.

For further information on
Blackwell Publishing, visit our website:
www.blackwellpublishing.com

Contents

List of Illustrations   vii

Series Editors' Preface   viii

Acknowledgments   x

1   Entering the Territory of Territory   1
    Introduction   1
    The Social Life of Territory   10
    Practical Definitions and a Grammar of Territory   13
    What Is Territory For?   18
    Seeing Around and Through Territory   20
    Concluding Remarks   33

2   Disciplining and Undisciplining Territory   34
    Introduction   34
    Territory and its Disciplines   35
    Deterritorializing the Disciplines   51
    Concluding Remarks   69

3   *Human Territoriality* and its Boundaries   70
    Introduction   70
    Overview   72
    Beyond *Human Territoriality*   86

4   Parsing Palisraelestine   102
    Introduction   102
    The Unfolding of Sovereignties   105
    Reconfiguring Property   124

The Israeli Territorial System of Control   132
Concluding Remarks   144

5   Further Explorations   146
    Books   147
    Topical Works   149
    Journals   150
    The Internet   151

    Bibliography   153

    Index   163

Illustrations

Figures

In chapter 1

The edge of sovereignty: Canada (Quebec)–US (Vermont) border   24
The edge of jurisdiction: Massachusetts–New York state line   24
The edge of the local state: Sand Lake, New York   25
Conditions of entry: US Federal Arsenal, Watervliet, New York   25
"Never Mind the Dog": private residence, Santa Barbara, California   26
Territoriality in the workplace   26

Maps

In chapter 4

1   Palestine under Ottoman rule   106
2   The Sykes–Picot partition   112
3   United Nations Recommendation for a two-states solution in
    Palestine, 1947   115
4   Armistice Line of 1949   117
5   Israeli conquests, 1967   120
6   Interim Israeli–Palestinian agreement, 1994   122

Series Editors' Preface

Short Introductions to Geography are highly accessible books, written by leading scholars, that are designed to introduce key geographical ideas to students and other interested readers. Departing from a traditional sub-disciplinary review, they seek to explain and explore central geographical and spatial concepts. These concise introductions convey a sense of the intellectual liveliness, differing perspectives, and key debates that have developed around each concept. Readers are also encouraged to think in new and critical ways about concepts that are core to geographical study. The series serves a vital pedagogic function, encouraging students to recognize how concepts and empirical analyses develop together and in relation to each other. Instructors meanwhile will be assured that students have an essential conceptual reference point, which they can supplement with their own examples and discussion. The short, modular format for the series allows instructors to combine two or more of these texts in a single class, or to use the text across classes with a distinctive sub-disciplinary focus.

Geraldine Pratt

Nicholas Blomley

For those who are unjustly excluded,
expelled, confined, or invaded

Acknowledgments

I would like to thank Nick Blomley and Gerry Pratt for inviting me to participate in the Short Introduction series. I would also like to thank Simon Alexander, Tim Cresswell, Michele Emanatian, Baruch Kimmerling, Kelvin Matthews, Janet Moth, Anssi Paasi, Bob Sack, Dmitri Sidorov, Steve Silvern, Karen Underwood, and Justin Vaughan for support or inspiration along the way.

The editor and publisher gratefully acknowledge the permission granted to reproduce the following copyright material in this book:

Anderson, E., "The Sykes–Picot partition," from *The Middle East: Geography and Geopolitics*, 8th edn (London: Routledge, 2000), p. 104. Used with permission of Routledge.

Bornstein A., "The Armistice line of 1949" and "Interim Israeli–Palestinian agreement, 1994," from *Crossing the Green Line Between the West Bank and Israel* (Philadelphia: University of Pennsylvania Press, 2002), pp. 31–2. Used with permission of the University of Pennsylvania Press.

Bregman A., "Israeli conquests, 1967," from *Israel's Wars: A History Since 1947* (London: Routledge, 2000), p. 94. Used with permission of Routledge.

Kimmerling B., and Migdal J., "Palestine under Ottoman rule," and "United Nations Recommendation for a two-states solution in Palestine, 1947," from *The Palestinian People: A History* (Cambridge, MA: Harvard University Press; Cartography Department, Hebrew University, 2003), pp. 33, 139. Used with permission of Harvard University Press and the authors.

Every effort has been made to trace copyright holders and to obtain their permission for the use of copyright material. The publisher apologizes for any errors or omissions in the above list and would be grateful if notified of any corrections that should be incorporated in future reprints or editions of this book.

I

Entering the Territory
of Territory

Introduction

Nothing better reveals how something is supposed to work than when it isn't working. Territory is no exception. Territory, according to common understandings, promotes peace through certainty by clearly defining and delineating the workings of power. In international relations we are "sovereign" on this side of the line and they are sovereign on the other side. With respect to land tenure or property I may plant corn on this side of the fence and you may graze cattle on the other side. In the context of privacy I may close my door and play with my Barbie dolls and all the world is obligated to stay outside. With clear lines, misunderstandings don't turn into disputes as easily and disputes don't escalate into fights. As we all know, good fences make good neighbors.

In the late winter/early spring of 2003 more than 100,000 American and British soldiers – and their associated equipment of guns, jets, supplies, and journalists – assembled on the Kuwaiti side of the Iraq–Kuwait border in preparation for the invasion of Iraq that would remove Saddam Hussein from power and result in the long-term occupation of the country. The power to grant or withhold permission for the US to use the territorial spaces of Kuwait, Qatar, and other nation-states as places from which to launch the invasion is itself a sovereign prerogative. And, in fact, the original battle plan was to invade Iraq simultaneously from the north, but at the last moment the Turkish parliament refused to allow the use of its territory for this purpose (Purdum et al. 2003). So had Saudi Arabia, at least formally. The principle of territorial integrity – by which is meant the absence of territorial violation – is one of the most fundamental principles of international law. It is also, as is well known, one which is not always respected. There are many ways in which territorial integrity can be compromised, but the most obvious and devastating are those involving the means of destruction associated with modern warfare. However one may have felt about it as the images of the American "Shock and Awe" campaign were broadcast around the world, and however it may have been rhetorically justified, the invasion and occupation of Iraq is a rather clear example of territory – or territory of a particular kind – not working as it is supposed to.

But, one rationale might go, that invasion was simply the unavoidable result of the invasion of Kuwait 12 years earlier by the armies of Iraq. In the first Gulf War the United States repelled the invaders. As part of the settlement of that war the government of Iraq was required to admit United Nations weapons inspectors who were authorized to investigate the presence of weapons of mass destruction (Sifry and Cerf 2003). Severe economic sanctions were also imposed on "Iraq" – which is to say, on the people of Iraq. These resulted in the deaths of tens of thousands more, many of whom were children (Hiro 2001; Research Unit for Political Economy 2003). The victors of the first Gulf War also imposed "no-fly zones" in the northern and southern sections of the country and periodically shot down Iraqi planes that violated these territorial prohibitions. At the beginning of the 2003 war Iraq was hardly the prototypic sovereign state and its territorial integrity was, at best, theoretical.

The 1991 Iraqi invasion of Kuwait was given rhetorical justification by Saddam Hussein through reference to the putative illegitimacy of the partitioning of the Ottoman province of Basra by the British when they invented "Iraq" and "Kuwait" in the early twentieth century (Dodge 2003; Finnie 1992). And *those* episodes of territorial invention were but sideshows to the Great Power geopolitics attending the aftermath of World War I, the maintenance of empire, and the emerging rivalries concerning the control of petroleum in an industrial order for which it had become life's blood. Preceding the invasion of Kuwait, Iraq, this time with the support of the United States, had fought a brutal war with Iran. The 2003 invasion took place, then, not just across a line drawn in the sand but within the historical context of a succession of territorializations and re-territorializations related to the control of oil and the wealth and power that this control generates. Looking at events with somewhat more historical depth, while in no way justifying them, serves the purpose of highlighting territoriality as a social (and political, economic, cultural) *process* that unfolds not only in place but through time. It thereby allows us to more easily see territories as social *products*. And learning to see *through* territory is valuable in learning to understand the world: the world as a whole and the worlds within which our lives are lived.

One of the more common explanations of territory – or, at least, the territorial state – is that it is a means of providing security to those "inside" from those ever-present dangers located "outside." And, undoubtedly, territory does often serve this purpose. But, when one considers the experiences of the hundreds of thousands of people whose lives have been violently terminated on the basis of claims rooted in the principle of territorial integrity in this part of the world in the last 30 years (a figure that would include the hundreds of thousands of casualties from the Iran–Iraq war of 1980–1988, and the genocidal massacre of Kurdish people by the Iraqi state), and adds these to the millions of others killed on the strength of similar justifications, these common explanations become at least a bit questionable. If this is "security" one might reasonably wonder what insecurity would feel like. In the twentieth century, a time when the territorial nation-state achieved global hegemony as the sole "legitimate" political institution, more than 100 million people were killed in wars, many of them directly concerned with, or at least given rhetorical justification with reference to, territory.

Or, consider happenings at another border, that separating the sovereign territories of the United States and Mexico. This border and these territories also have a very complicated history. Most of the present border was given formal legal expression in the treaty of Guadalupe Hidalgo of 1848 (Frazier 1998). This treaty ended what Americans call the Mexican War. Like the Iraqi invasion of Kuwait, this war 150 years earlier was simply a method by which the government of one nation-state attempted to annex to itself the territory of another, and with no better justification. But unlike the more recent event, in this case the invaded state (Mexico) was not aided by a global superpower, and the invading state (the United States) prevailed. Its manifest destiny, its unquestionable supremacy, were validated on the field of battle, and the map of sovereignty was redrawn. The border shifted hundreds of miles southward and people and things that had been "in" Mexico now found themselves "in" the United States. Newly included were thousands of Mexican citizens. As contemporary Chicano activists say, "We didn't cross the border, the border crossed us" (Acuña 1996, 109). It also included dozens of indigenous peoples such as the Apache, Hopi, Navajo, and Shoshone people, who were involuntarily – if only partially – subjected to the workings of American sovereignty because of their location vis-à-vis this shifting border. It also included the gold, lumber, and real estate of California.

With respect to the contemporary border there is what many people describe as another, and perhaps more insidious, "invasion" taking place. William Griggs writes, "While American troops engage al-Qaeda in terrorist cells in far-flung battlefields across Asia and our military leadership prepares for a Gulf war encore against Iraq, our 'friend' and 'neighbor' to the South is relentlessly invading our homeland" (2002, 21).

In his view, "The Mexican government, radical Chicano separatists, and the Bush administration all agree on one thing: the border separating our nation from Mexico should be treated as if it does not exist" (2002, 21). Hundreds of thousands of workers cross the border from south to north every week under conditions that are formally prohibited but are in other ways tolerated or encouraged. But they must do so surreptitiously, sneaking around or tunneling beneath the border (Martinez 2001). While countless thousands succeed in crossing over, finding work, or being reunited with family, many are apprehended and sent back to the other side only to make the attempt again and again. Many men, women, and children die of thirst and exposure in the deserts or suffocate in the trucks and train cars used to smuggle them inside (Egan 2004). In fact, during 2002–3 roughly the same number of Mexican workers died trying to cross over as American soldiers were killed before victory was declared in the war with Iraq (US Department of State 2004). Religious organizations such as Humane Borders have established programs to leave water in places that the Mexican and Central American sojourners can find (www.humaneborders.org). At the same time, organizations such as Ranch Rescue have established armed vigilante groups that conduct paramilitary operations to patrol the border in defense of property and sovereignty (www.ranchrescue.com). The border is not simply a line on a map. It and the territories it marks and separates are conditions of living and dying.

These are, admittedly, rather extreme illustrations. While there are always a certain number of wars and border disputes taking place on the planet, military invasions of the magnitude of the American war in Iraq are comparatively rare. Likewise, few border regions have the volatile mix of features that characterizes the US–Mexico borderlands. But, extreme as these situations may be, they do at least demonstrate that the significance of territory in the modern world cannot be underestimated. They also suggest that this significance concerns both how social relations are organized on a planetary scale and how the lives of countless individuals are caught up, one way or another, with the dynamics of modern territoriality. And this, of course, is everyone.

These two examples only scratch the surface. Each is concerned with only one form of territory, that associated with the political institution of the modern nation-state. The key discourses according to which this kind of territory is made intelligible include international relations, international law, and geopolitics. But the 200 or so territorial spaces that constitute the international system of states do not exhaust the forms that territory takes in the modern world. Actually, depending on one's theoretical perspective and the fineness of one's analysis, there are potentially billions of territories, large and small. There are innumerable complex territorial configurations and assemblages that shape human social life, relationships, and interactions. On the "inside" of states are numerous political and administrative subdivisions, preserves, zones, districts, precincts, parishes, and areas. There are also countless property lots, apartments, rooms, offices, cells, and camps. The list is endless. Overarching and embracing the territoriality of nation-states are many supra-national, multinational, and international territories created by treaties or conventions, such as the European Union or the North American Free Trade Area. Territory may find expression in the space embracing NATO membership and in the tow-away zone in front of the grocery store; in parks, prisons, and club houses; in workplaces, gang turfs, and multinational business organizations. With respect to each of these it matters if you are "in" or "out." For most people, perhaps, the micro-territories of everyday life may be more significant – or at least more noticeable, than the macro-territories of global politics.

Let's think small for a moment. Begin where you are. Look around at the ways in which the social spaces you are occupying give form to your days. Consider the rooms you have access to and those from which you are excluded – or are allowed to enter only with permission. In a social order in which private property is a fundamental feature, most of the world of daily experience is closed off to you. This world is also territorialized with reference to public and private spaces. Imagine how shifts in this public/private configuration would affect your daily life. Imagine, for example, that many of the "public" spaces through which the paths of your days unwind were "privatized" and the terms of your access or exclusion made to depend on your ability to pay or on whatever the new "owners" chose to condition your entry. (In order to help flesh out this thought experiment consider the differences between a "traditional" small town's main street and a contemporary shopping mall.) Imagine further that entry is made conditional on what you look like: white? female? young? This is territoriality at work. On the other hand, imagine that what you take to be private space – *your* private space, your home, your bedroom – were to be opened up to continuous governmental surveillance and the images produced broadcast on television. This too would constitute a fairly significant form of territorial revision. Now imagine both, a social order in which "public" and "private" as we know them have ceased to be a fundamental way of territorializing social life.

Or consider this. Ray Oliver owned a farm near Jamestown, Kentucky. "He had," according to US Supreme Court Justice Lewis Powell, "posted No Trespassing signs at regular intervals and had locked the gate at the entrance to the center of the farm" (466 U.S. 170 1983, 173). One day two Kentucky State policemen, acting on a tip, drove onto Oliver's land, past his house, and up to the locked gate. Disregarding both the No Trespassing sign and shouted orders from someone in the distance to "get out," they walked around the gate and into a wooded area on Oliver's land. About a mile from Oliver's house, in a spot surrounded on all sides by trees, they found marijuana growing. The policemen left, went back to town to obtain a search warrant from a judge, and then returned to the Oliver place to arrest him. In American law the police had not only trespassed, they had violated Oliver's constitutionally protected rights of privacy, or, at least, that is what his attorney argued at his trial. The fourth amendment of the US Constitution prohibits government agents from conducting warrantless searches, or at least it seems to. The Supreme Court has on numerous occasions declared that illegally obtained evidence (that is, evidence of a crime acquired in violation of the fourth amendment) is to be excluded from criminal trials. This is called the fruit of the poison tree doctrine. The trial court agreed with Oliver's lawyer. Oliver "had done all that could be expected of him to assert his privacy in the area of the farm to be searched" (p. 173) and the police had acted illegally by searching first and securing a warrant only after the search proved successful. The case was duly dismissed.

The government, however, appealed and a higher court reversed the judgment. The US Supreme Court agreed to hear the case and decided that the tree was not poisoned after all. Fourth amendment protections, reasoned the majority, only apply to a person's home and the area immediately surrounding the home (a space called the curtilage). Only "certain enclaves should be free from arbitrary government interference," the majority asserted (p. 178). Locks and signs notwithstanding, other areas on one's property are therefore vulnerable to arbitrary government interference and searching in these places does not require a warrant. These areas are called "open fields," even though, as Justice Lewis Powell explained, "an open field need be neither 'open' nor a 'field' as those terms are used in common speech" (p. 180). And because this secluded location surrounded by trees was an "open field" it could not be shielded from public view and the property owner did not have a reasonable expectation of privacy there. And so, the evidence of the crime ought not to have been excluded nor the case dismissed.

But other Supreme Court justices didn't see it this way. Oliver's space (and his rights), in their view, had been invaded by the government and the police were guilty of criminal trespass. Quoting Justice Powell's remarks from another case, Justice Thurgood Marshall wrote,

> [o]ne of the main rights attaching to property is the right to exclude others
> ... one who owns ... property will ... have a legitimate expectation of privacy by virtue of this right to exclude. Governmental agents without a warrant

– absent an emergency – are no less excludable than anyone else. These rights and expectations are made stronger by the signs and locks ... [B]y marking the boundaries of the land with warnings that the public should not intrude, the owner has dispelled any ambiguity as to his desires. (p. 195)

For the dissenters, as well as for the trial judge, Keep Out means keep out. But, unfortunately for Ray Oliver and the countless others whose property is now vulnerable to warrantless searches on the authority of this case, Justice Marshall was writing a dissenting opinion, not a majority opinion.

We will have occasion to return to Ray Oliver's case later in this chapter. For now the point to be emphasized is that territory and territoriality do not implicate only issues of international boundaries and international relations. In Oliver's story there are many territories in play. Looked at one way the case is about the (re)territorialization of public and private. Looked at another way it is about the (re)territorialization of the relationship between property and constitutional federalism in the United States. Looked at in detail the case is about reconfiguring the territorial relationships among "home," "the curtilage," and "open fields" – or, rather, using these notions to restructure the relationship between territory, power, and experience. However we slice it, the way these territories are understood (by owners, policemen, and judges) is consequential. For Ray Oliver it may have made the difference between going to prison or not.

Consider another property case. Wallace Mason kept homing pigeons in a coop in his backyard. But someone had been breaking into the coop and stealing his pigeons. So one "dark, rainy night," seeing dark figures in his yard, he fired his shotgun at the invaders (159 So. 2d 700 1964, 701). He hit 14-year-old Michael McKellar and his friend, 13-year-old Leo Schnell. Michael was hit in the back and was paralyzed for the rest of his life. Mason was not arrested or charged with a crime but Michael's father sued Mason. The trial court dismissed the suit and McKellar appealed to the Louisiana Supreme Court. The majority of that court declared that

> Mason's act in shooting the two thieves, while not completely justified is excusable ... We are not prepared to say that he exceeded his rights in protecting his domain. The Constitutions of the United States and Louisiana give us the right to keep and bear arms. It follows, logically, that to keep and bear arms gives us the right to use them for the intended purpose for which they were manufactured. A man's home has traditionally been his castle, and he who enters therein with felonious intent does so at his own peril. (pp. 703–4)

Mason was simply protecting his property. And given "the history of previous invasions of his property" (p. 703), he was fully justified in shooting the invaders. But, as with the Oliver case, another judge saw things differently and dissented. The dissenting judge took note of other facts of the matter. Mason was an experienced hunter and evidence suggested that he had been lying in wait. Most importantly, there was "no doubt that the two boys were trying to escape when they were shot." Both boys had been shot in the back. "Mason knew they were going, even running, in the direction away from the house," and Schnell "was going over the fence when [Mason] shot him" (p. 706).

Just as territory was made meaningful in the Oliver case with reference to legal notions such as "open fields" and "curtilage," so this case was informed by legal notions such as "the castle doctrine" (that is, that use of force is justified in defending one's "castle") and the duty to retreat. When one is threatened with violence in public one has a duty to retreat before responding with violence in self-defense. But when one is on one's property the castle doctrine overrides the duty to retreat. If Mason had shot at the boys before they climbed his fence he most likely would have been charged with committing mayhem – or worse. But crossing the line transforms the legal significance of the event. It therefore transforms the practical significance of the event: what it meant to the kids, to Mason, and to the authoritative interpreters of territory. Again, *this is the difference that territory makes.* As with some of my earlier illustrations, this is rather dramatic. But even if events like these are common enough they are not everyday occurrences for most of us. The general point holds for events that are much more common, such as run-of-the-mill evictions and detentions as well as non-evictions and non-detentions. Both of these property cases reveal important aspects of how territory works in the world of experience.

Instances of the practical significance of territory for how everyday life is experienced can be multiplied indefinitely. This raises a number of issues that it is the objective of this Short Introduction to address. One question immediately suggests itself: given the vast variety of forms that territory can assume – as merely suggested by the examples presented so far – can anything useful be said about territory and territoriality *as such* apart from the countless forms they take and the limitless ends to which they are a means? Put another way, are the diverse social practices associated with territoriality in connection with, say, wars among nation-states, the privacy rights of landowners, the allocation of garden plots in Swaziland, or the rules concerning access to a college dormitory room all examples of the same phenomenon such that generalizations can be made that apply as easily to one context as to the others? Or, might it be the case that the same *word* is simply being used for what are better seen as very different sorts of things? If the latter is the case, then perhaps the attempt to treat them as if they were the same sort of thing is, at best, an inappropriate and unproductive abstraction. In the following discussion I will proceed by attempting both to keep the question open (and acknowledge that territory in connection with the invasion of Iraq and territory in connection with a teenager's bedroom have less in common than use of the same word might suggest) and to assume for practical purposes that there *is* something useful to say about territory *per se*. Part of my reason for adopting this approach is that, with few notable exceptions, there is a strong tendency for territory to be discussed and theorized as if the different forms and manifestations were not even related phenomena. Studies of macro- and micro-territorial structures and configurations and of those "in between" tend to be uninformed by each other.

As I will discuss more fully in chapter 2, territory has, until recently, tended to be studied by different academic disciplines predominantly as a comparatively simple aspect of the more central concerns of those disciplines. For instance, it is commonly regarded as an aspect of sovereignty in international relations theory, as an expression of collective identity in anthropology, and as a means toward the promotion of privacy or emotional security in environmental psychology. Even in human geography, the discipline in which one might expect territory to be assessed more as a phenomenon in its own right, it has most often been examined within the sub-disciplinary domain of political geography and therefore relegated to questions about the workings of nation-states. The academic propensity to "territorialize" territory – and to subordinate it to what are conventionally taken to be each discipline's real core concerns – has had the paradoxical effect of marginalizing it as a topic in its own right. This disciplinary territorialization (and marginalization) of territory is quite understandable. However, it has had the effect of closing off a number of questions before they have been raised and of obscuring a number of connections that a more catholic approach might draw attention to. More to the point, most disciplinary treatments of territory simply – actively – *assume* the questions closed, and thereby insufficiently problematize territory. In the following pages, then, I will be assuming that there are some general and useful things that can be said about territory. One of the most important is this: territory is commonly understood as a device for simplifying and clarifying something else, such as political authority, cultural identity, individual autonomy, or rights. In order to have this effect territory *itself* has to be taken as a relatively simple and clear phenomenon. But as I will suggest throughout the present book, territory is anything but simple and clear. As the brief illustrations I've given so far suggest, it is an extremely complex and often highly ambiguous element of social life, relationships, and interactions. Consequently, the best way to clarify the practical workings of territoriality is to initially complicate our common-sense understandings.

The Social Life of Territory

Territories are human social creations. Although territoriality, like language, may, in some very general sense, be a human universal, also like language, the specific forms that it takes are enormously varied. Territoriality is an important element of how human associations – cultures, societies, smaller collectives – and institutions organize themselves in space. It is an aspect of how individual humans as embodied beings organize themselves with respect to the social and material world. Territories, then, are significant cultural artifacts of a rather special kind. As with any artifacts – shrunken heads, scepters, bowling balls, cluster bombs – territories reflect and incorporate features of the social order that creates them. Stone Age manifestations of territoriality were certainly different from electronic age manifestations of territoriality. The territories of literate societies differ from those of oral societies insofar as these involve strongly dissimilar forms of social life and different kinds of communicative practices. How territory manifests itself among people whose primary economic activity is fairly localized hunting and gathering differs in important ways from those of agriculturalists as these, in turn, differ from the manifestations of territoriality in a global capitalist, industrial social order. Political liberalism is territorialized differently than are fascist police states. This is all to say that territories are not simple artifacts by any means. Rather, they are fundamentally *constitutive* of the social orders whose features they express. One might go so far as to say that a cultural formation or social order is unintelligible without reference (if only tacit) to how it is territorially expressed. This being the case, any significant revision of the terms of territorialization (such as with respect to public and private) entails an equally significant social transformation (and vice versa).

This general theme can be seen by reflection on any of the world historic processes that are associated with the emergence, continual transformation, and global diffusion of specifically modern forms of territory. Looked at globally, if far too abstractly, the long, uneven demise of European feudalism, the processes of European-derived imperialism and colonialism, of decolonization and related nationalisms, the global saturation of the territorial nation-state, the rise and fall of state socialism, the wars and resistances through which these have been given material force, etc. all entailed the continuous (if uneven) re-territorialization of social life. And these abstract "processes" and "forces" have all played out on the ground in ways that have profoundly shaped the rhythms, experiences, relationships, and consciousness of ordinary people. Many of the most obvious forms of identity and ways of being that characterize modernity are directly tied to these seemingly ceaseless territorial operations. The citizen, the settler, the alien, the native, the owner, the tenant, the prisoner, the manager, the refugee, the squatter, and countless others are among the territorialized social roles and figures who inhabit our world. These are among the social roles and figures that we *are*. And because these figures are *relational* – that is, because they are what they are in relation to others – they reflect the complex territorialization of networks of social relationships. So while perhaps one may be able to make generalizations about territory *per se*, one ought not conceive of it as in any way separate from the history of the social, at least insofar as the social is what it is, in part, through how it is territorialized. If it makes sense to say that cultures create or "produce" territories, they do so through the process of reproducing and re-creating themselves. (Or, of course, they may be transformed by the imposition of novel forms of territory by others.)

As I have already suggested, one important aspect of how territoriality commonly works is through its being regarded in a rather taken-for-granted way as an almost natural phenomenon. To the extent that territory (e.g. nationalist territory, or private property) appears to be self-evident, necessary, or unquestionable, it may obscure the play of power and politics in its formation and maintenance. Actions based on or in furtherance of territory may be easily justified by "communal" or universalizing claims. But, to the extent that it – or any given manifestation of it – is seen as contingent, socially constructed, ideologically informed, and, when push comes to shove, enforced by physical violence, then the forms of power which are inherently connected to territory may become more visible, and justifications, more clearly partial or partisan.

Of course, particular territorializations are commonly contested. International boundary disputes, arguments about whether a given action counts as a trespass or whether a particular eviction is justified by the rules, fights over the allocation of garden plots among villagers, and so on are everyday occurrences. But for territory to "work" effectively *the basic principles* of territoriality cannot be seriously questioned. When they are, as when private ownership of land is questioned, when colonial powers displace indigenous peoples, when existing political communities are partitioned, when racialized territories such as those associated with Jim Crow or apartheid are attacked, then the contingencies of territory are more clearly revealed and the claims that these territorializations are necessary or natural features of our life-worlds are more easily discounted. Territorial configurations are not simply cultural artifacts. They are political achievements.

Territoriality, then, is much more than a strategy for control of space. It is better understood as implicating and being implicated in ways of thinking, acting, and being in the world – ways of world-making informed by beliefs, desires, and culturally and historically contingent ways of knowing. It is as much a metaphysical phenomenon as a material one. Territory, in turn, informs key aspects of collective and individual identities. It shapes and is shaped by collective social and self-consciousness. In social orders predicated on conflict and contradiction and characterized by a relatively large degree of reflexive thought, not only are these conflicts and contradictions reflected in that society's territorial configurations, they are also subject to a variety of imaginative re-visionings and a multifaceted politics of territory. Some aspects of the politics of territory may directly concern the territorial state or its subdivisions. Many do not, or do so less directly. These include territorial conflicts of "private life" involving issues of race, gender, age, and so on, or those within families, communities, institutions, and workplaces.

One of the aims of this Short Introduction is to sketch out some of the complexity of territory and to give more than the usual attention to its contingent character. Ideally, this is a four-step process. First, we need to *see* territory and the commonplace workings of territoriality all around us. Second, we need to *see around* territory, to contextualize it and trace its connections to other social phenomena. Third, we need to *see through* territory to reveal what is commonly obscured by the default naturalizing discourses such as those centered on sovereignty, jurisdiction, and property. And finally, a fourth step is to imagine *seeing past* extant forms of territory and to imagine other, perhaps better – or, perhaps, much worse – ways of territorializing social life on this planet.

To these ends the present chapter is a further introduction to the very idea of territory that emphasizes features that are, I believe, commonly obscured by more conventional understandings. In the remainder of the chapter I first offer what I will call a *grammar of territory*. This is an analysis which will allow us to see territories as more than static, inert things and instead focuses on the dynamic social processes and practices through and in relation to which territorial forms emerge or are transformed. This is followed by a brief discussion of the posited functions of territory – what territory does or is imagined to accomplish. The main objective is to be able to think critically about approaches to territory that simply assume or articulate a small number of pseudo-natural functions and to suggest a more pragmatic conception. Far from being a timeless, universal feature of human social existence, territory is deeply historical (and historically contingent) in a number of ways. The next section narrows the discussion to the relationship between territory and the historical epoch of modernity. The dynamic nature of modernity and its character of continuous transformation is stressed here. A related factor, the increase in mobility of people, things, and ideas characteristic of modernity, is also discussed. Next I touch on the interpretability of territory. Territory necessarily conveys meanings but these meanings are often open to various interpretations. Modern territory, in particular, is often textually represented (as discussion of the Oliver and McKellar cases demonstrated), and even the most obvious of meanings (Keep Out, Whites Only) can be *re*interpreted in light of what are taken to be controlling texts such as legal statutes or constitutions or in light of competing interpretive frameworks. Much of the dynamism of modern territory is related to this textuality and interpretability. Finally I will briefly discuss the "verticality" of modern territory, or the complex relations among overlapping territorial entities. Through the metaphor of verticality we are commonly asked to imagine that we occupy a nested set of discrete territories simultaneously (rooms, buildings, local communities, states or regions, nation-states). Often, though, the "meanings" of one territorial element are in tension (or can be brought into tension) with those of another, and there ensue arguments about the line that distinguishes one from the other, arguments about which set of meanings has primacy in the event of a conflict. How these metaphorical "boundary disputes" between vertically related spaces play out is also an extremely important aspect of the politics of modern territory.

Practical Definitions and a Grammar of Territory

One useful exercise for learning to see through territory is to consider its grammar, or the syntax, semantics, and pragmatics of the cluster of words centered on "territory." Territory, of course, is a noun. But restricting attention to territory as a noun may have the effect of over-emphasizing its apparent "thingness" and thereby neglecting its relationship to a range of other social phenomena, most especially the social activities, practices, and processes that are implicated in its production and transformation. This grammatical exercise aims to correct this common imbalance. Before that, though, it might be useful to say something about the etymology of the term. One common etymology derives "territory" from the Latin word *territorium* "the land around a town" and *terra* or land. However, as William Connolly (1996) suggests, the roots of "territory" may be more interesting.

> *Terra* means land, earth, nourishment, sustenance; it conveys the sense of a sustaining medium, solid, fading off into indefiniteness. But the form of the word, the [*Oxford English Dictionary*] says, suggests that it derives from *terrere*, meaning to frighten, to terrorize. And *Territorium* is a "place from which people are warned." Perhaps these two contending derivations continue to occupy territory today. To occupy a territory is to receive sustenance and to exercise violence. Territory is land occupied by violence. (p. 144)

This suggests that territory is contentious in its very roots.

As a first approximation, *a* territory – regarded in isolation, as is often the case in definitions – is a bounded social space that inscribes a certain sort of meaning onto defined segments of the material world. A simple territory marks a differentiation between an "inside" and an "outside." The meanings refer, in the first instance, to the practical significance of being on the *in*side or the *out*side or of crossing the line that distinguishes one side from the other. The line may distinguish a passer-by from a trespasser, or an alien from a citizen. The basics of territory, then, are fairly straightforward: a space, a line, some meaning, some state of affairs. Having said this, however, countless variables suggest themselves. Some territories are rather enduring, others are quite ephemeral. Some are formal, while others are informal. Territories such as the territorial nation-state aspire to near total reference or relevance to what is "inside," while others, such as the sales territories of a sporting goods company, may be of very limited relevance or have significance for rather few people. The parish-diocese-archdiocese structure of the Roman Catholic Church may be very important for bishops, priests, and parishioners but have very little relevance for non-Catholics.

The boundary of a territory may be expressed by physical structures – fences, walls, gates, or doors. Or it may be announced by linguistic signs – "Bienvenue du Quebec," "Authorized Personnel Only," "MEN," "Keep Off the Grass." But these are not necessary. In fact, for more informal or ephemeral territories they may be impossible, or at least impractical. The point here is that a territory and its boundary are *meaningful*. They are significant insofar as they signify. What a given territory means – the specific terms of difference, limit, access, exclusion, the consequences attached to crossing a line – depends on the kind of social relationships it is implicated with. For example, international boundary lines carry different kinds of meanings than property lines (even if they coincide in location), or the thresholds of office cubicles, or the boundaries of a sales territory. Unauthorized incursions into a co-worker's cubicle may be grounds for disciplinary action but not grounds for a military reprisal. In important ways, of course, every specific boundary line carries a unique set of meanings. The Syria–Israel boundary conveys meaning that the Norway–Sweden boundary does not. The point is that, before we can discuss *what* a territory means, or *how* it is made meaningful, it needs to be emphasized *that* it means. If a territory is a kind of thing, an artifact, it is a meaningful thing, an artifact that is understood as "containing" and "conveying" various sorts of meaning. Territories are not only spatial entities but also communicative devices.

A territory is a bounded meaningful space, whether that space is called China or the common area of a condominium or the Diocese of Albany. *Territoriality* refers more to the relationship between territories *and some other social phenomena*. It draws attention to the territorial aspects, conditions, or implications of something else. So, the territoriality of state authority focuses on the spatial aspect of formal political power. Reference to the territoriality of racism, as this was expressed under apartheid or in many contemporary urban settings, allows one to discern the constitutive involvement of territorial structures in how racism works and is experienced. Examination of the territoriality of work would highlight the processes of segmentation or integration of labor by means of territorial reconfigurations. Territoriality, understood in this *relational* sense, treats territory less like an inert "thing" and more as an aspect of various dimensions of social life. It helps us to shift our attention to the social phenomena of interest. We can, therefore, analyze the territoriality of institutions (schools, prisons, hospitals), of organizations (corporations, military, religions), of activities (child's play, money laundering, drug use), or of aspects of identity or social being. Moreover, the term *territoriality* can also be modified to focus on more specific relationships or processes: the gendered territoriality of child's play, the racialized territoriality of political representation. This allows us to examine how territoriality is implicated in the social expression of these sorts of connections; how, for example, territory mediates the interplay of gender and age, or race and political power.

As the shift from *territory* to *territoriality* brings different relationships more clearly into view, so a related shift from nouns to the verb forms derived from territory bring social practices and processes more clearly into view. In recent years a number of scholars have written about the de-territorial*ization* or re-territorial*ization* of state power under conditions of global*ization*. These "-ization" terms are also nouns, but they are formed from the process verbs *territorialize* and *globalize*. While rather unwieldy, these verb forms draw attention to territoriality as an activity and to territories as the *products* of social practices and processes. As transitive verbs they imply objects. Thus we can understand the emergence of Jim Crow racial segregation in the United States of the nineteenth century as a particular territorialization of race (or, more accurately, the territorialization of power on the basis of race), and desegregation in the 1950s to 1970s as the relative de-territorialization of power on the basis of race.

These verbs also often imply a subject, an individual or collective agent who engages in territorial practices in relation to others. Often these activities entail deliberation, intentionality, or strategy, but this is not necessary insofar as some territorial configurations may be the unintended or unforeseen consequences of other social forces or processes or the aggregate effect of numerous specific territorializations. In any case, "to territorialize" is to deploy territory in a particular context by linking some phenomenon or entity to a meaningful bounded space. For example, political representation can be territorialized through the creation of voting districts, or de-territorialized through proportional representation or at-large schemes. But actions such as these are often a matter of degree insofar as de-territorialization on one scale entails a re-territorialization on another scale. (For example, a shift from a representation scheme based on districts to one based on at-large apportioning is still territorial.) To emphasize territorializing *practices* situates territory more firmly within the realm of social action. Few, if any, human territories simply appear outside of the play of general social processes and specific social practices. Territorial nation-states do not just come into being and fade away. The continual re-territorialization of labor is not a natural process like evolution or seasonality. If territories are artifacts, they are produced under specific historical and social conditions. This fairly obvious fact can easily be obscured by confining one's analysis to "territory" as such.

This grammatical exploration of the conceptual domain of territory is useful for keeping some of the complexities of the topic in mind. What bears emphasizing here in our attempt to see around, through, and past territory is that territory cannot be considered apart from two fundamental aspects of human social being: meaning and power and the contingencies of their relationship. Whatever else one might say about it, territory necessarily involves the workings of some form of social power. Power itself, though, is quite a complex social phenomenon (Lukes 1986). It may be oppressive, coercive, asymmetric and constraining or emancipatory, benign or enabling. Its expression may be interpersonal and very localized or global and impersonal. The reasons for its exercise may be malicious, altruistic, or indifferent. It may be contradictory and tension-laden or co-operative. The point is that when we look *through* territory what we will always see are constellations of social relational power. Territory may facilitate or impede the workings of power, control, self-determination, or solidarity. Territorializations are the expressions of power, and of how power is manifested in the material world. This fundamental relationship to social power is one of the features that distinguishes territory from other forms of social space. Throughout this book the inextricable yet complex and shifting connections between territory and power are axiomatic.

Territoriality is also implicated in the creation, circulation, and interpretation of meaning. I will return to this theme later in this chapter. For now it is enough to say that territory always signifies. "Meaning," of course, is no less complex a social phenomenon than power. Giving due consideration to power, meaning, and space in combination begins to give some sense of the complexity of even the simplest territory. This constitutive relationship to meaning also distinguishes territories from other spatial forms. Not every enclosed space is a territory. What makes an enclosed space a territory is, first, that it signifies, and, second, that the meanings it carries or conveys refer to or implicate social power. But meaning and power are not independent of each other. In assessing the inscription of meaning to a space – or to the line defining the space and differentiating it from other spaces – one might reasonably inquire about the power to create and assign these meanings in the first place. For example, a sign on a door reading "Whites Only" seems to carry an unambiguous meaning and seems to imply significant consequences for those who would disregard these meanings. In the United States, for generations such disregard would likely have resulted in the infliction of physical pain, humiliation, and anger. One way of understanding the Civil Rights movements of the 1950s and 1960s is as an effort to challenge not only the *meanings* of racialized territories but the *legitimacy* of the posited authority to impose such meanings onto social space and relationships.

Another dimension of the relationship between power and meaning in connection with territory that has received increasing attention concerns the relationship between territory and discourse more generally. I will return to this topic in subsequent chapters. For the present it is enough to say that the focus here would not be on this or that space but on the ideological, metaphorical, or metaphysical world-views or assumptions that make certain kinds of territories intelligible and the ways in which these representations are deployed in efforts to justify (or critique) the workings of power. An example that will be discussed more fully in chapter 2 is the discourse of geopolitics. This is a particular way of understanding and discussing the relationship between space and power in the context of international relations. It is an ideological-metaphysical complex that makes this sort of territorial mosaic make sense in a particular way. Important to the very ideas of "international relations" and "geopolitics" is a set of images and presuppositions (meanings) that treat "sovereign states" as if they were unified, autonomous subjects. The discourse of sovereignty, in turn, owes much of *its* sense-making capacity to an underlying image of personhood and rights. The discourses that make liberal forms of private property appear to be common-sense project similar meanings onto social space. Likewise, the territorializations of racial subordination have been inseparable from discourses of white supremacy or racial purity. The ways in which workplaces are territorialized are inextricable from ideologies of, say, efficiency, property, labor, and gender. In chapter 4 we will examine in some detail the relationship between territoriality and discourses of nationalism and Zionism in Israel/Palestine. The point here is that the justificatory (and critical) discourses that lie behind territorial processes and practices are as much a part of "the meanings" of a given space as the more obvious expressions such as "Keep Off the Grass," "Authorized Personnel Only," or "Bienvenue du Quebec." This grammatical excursion into the domain of territory, -iality, -ize, -ization, etc. is intended to help us situate the topic within social relationships and processes, the better to see it as a social-historical-political phenomenon.

In this Short Introduction I can only say so much about the constellation of space-power-meaning (and experience) that is "territory." What bears repeating is simply that these convergences and interrelations cannot be left out of considerations of territory, and that the workings of power and meaning in and through social space can neither be simply assumed as given nor bracketed off as irrelevant. The reason, again, is that *territory commonly works precisely through the tendency to take power and meaning and their relationship to be simply self-evident and rather non-problematic*. In this way, territory is reified and rendered as relatively simple and unambiguous. In this way territory does much of our thinking for us and closes off or obscures questions of power and meaning, ideology and legitimacy, authority and obligation, and how worlds of experience are continually made and remade.

What Is Territory For?

Some important questions that are commonly asked about territory (or of particular territories) are: What is it for? What are its functions? What does it do? One common set of answers proceeds from the assumption that human territoriality is somehow natural, that, in fact, it is a biological imperative. In this view the differences among the various expressions of territoriality, as exhibited by bluebirds, wasps, and human beings, are less significant than the similarities. So, just as the function of sex, however variously it is accomplished by different species, is *for* reproduction and genetic transmission, territoriality is simply *for* – a means to satisfying – some more basic and universal need. Often the posited need is the control of access to resources, whether these resources are acorns, nesting sites, oilfields, or sexual partners. This functional view of territory can implicate other posited needs such as dominance (reproductive or other) or self-preservation. For our purposes, though, this approach is not very helpful, insofar as it reduces an enormous range of phenomena and experiences to a very small number of posited functions. In so doing it marginalizes central questions of meaning and power. It also seems difficult to use this bluebird theory of territoriality to account for the vast variety in the forms that human territoriality has taken historically, cross-culturally, and, perhaps especially, under conditions of modernity. Territory may well be a human cultural universal, but like other universals, such as sex, work, family, or music, the forms that it takes in different cultural orders or historical periods vary enormously.

There are other more or less functional accounts, however, which acknowledge that human territoriality is radically other than non-human manifestations. Territory is not simply about sorting things in space for its own sake but is always a means to some other end – and these ends are by no means restricted to universal needs. Territory may be a solution to a problem. It may be a kind of strategy. Because territory always involves the communication of some sort of meaning and is essentially classificatory, it may have the function (or at least the effect) of reifying forms of identity and difference. It is very often a means of controlling what is "inside" the lines by limiting access or excluding others. As compared with other means of asserting control, territory may promote clarity and simplicity, and therefore certainty and predictability, and therefore peace, security and order, and therefore efficiency and progress. Some of these themes will be encountered in chapter 3.

While consideration of the functional virtues of territory may be useful, greater sensitivity toward the dynamics of power complicates the picture. Some aspects of social reality can be territorialized in ways that aggravate inefficiencies, breed resentment, or create patterns of dependence and subservience. More generally, in many cases the most obvious effect of territory is to disempower others: to divide and conquer, to confine or immobilize, to exclude, to create dependencies, to dilute power, to fragment and isolate. One might reasonably conclude that in many cases the function of territory is to *create* conflict or to exacerbate power asymmetries more or less for their own sake – or, for the sake of those whose interests are served by conflict or repression. The hyper-territorialization of racism, while not without relevance for the control of resources such as land and labor, seems to have been at least as much to give "race" a more concrete expression by reinforcing the terms of differential identities. To a large extent what it meant to be "white" under the spatial regimes of Jim Crow or apartheid was to have the power to say "whites only" and to trust that this mandate would be backed up by state violence. Functionalist understandings that assume that only good things follow from territorializations obscure some of the most significant effects of territory.

Functional approaches to territory *per se*, then, are not without difficulties. Perhaps all one can reasonably do is assess the functions – or, better, the myriad effects – of this or that type or instance of territoriality from this or that perspective. But again, many of the cumulative effects, or much of what territories do, may not have been intended by any particular actor. What may appear to be "functional" from one perspective may be dysfunctional – or worse – from other points of view. Also, territorial forms such as nation-states aspire to such a totalizing position that any manageable list of posited "functions" would be so abstract as to be of little value. I will return to this issue in chapter 3; for now it is enough to suggest that thinking about territory in terms of effects or consequences, whether or not these are intended or strategic, may open up lines of questioning that many conventional views close off.

Seeing Around and Through Territory

Territory and modernity

To this point I have been discussing territory in very general terms with little explicit reference to historical or cultural contexts. But seeing through territory requires that we situate its manifestations in their historical specificity. One set of distinctions that may be useful here is that between modernity and pre- (and, perhaps, post-) modernity. This, of course, introduces another layer of complexity, at least insofar as there are disputes about what features constitute the distinctions, that is, about what makes modernity "modern" (Bauman 2004). But this added element of complexity is productive if it can help us see through and past the territorial configurations within which our lives unfold. As an initial matter the distinction between modernity and pre-modernity is usually taken to be a temporal one. The pre-modern is commonly understood as before the present era. In contrast, the modern denotes a sort of continuing, if continually transforming, "now." The pre-modern may continue to exist in isolated pockets, but these are commonly understood as decreasing in number and significance. Modernity seems to be an inescapable future. But among the things that are commonly neglected in this formulation is the radical heterogeneity of "pre-modern" cultures. What makes them pre-modern is simply that they are *other than* modern – what they share is what they are not. But if we regard modernity as not simply a temporal condition or moment but a particular (and peculiar) sort of cultural formation, then we may see distinctively modern forms of territory in a different light.

For our immediate purpose of learning to see through and past the forms and practices that so profoundly affect our lives let me simply stipulate that "modernity" here refers to a particular way of life (an "episteme" or a culturally distinctive mode of thinking, feeling, and being) that began to emerge as a rather local cultural transformation in western Europe in the middle centuries of the second Christian millennium. Through the complex processes of imperialism, colonialism, world-wide capitalism, and literacy it came, in the middle decades of the twentieth century, to comprehensively, if quite unevenly, embrace the planet as a whole. It is associated with the appearance and global saturation of the international system of states (and associated bureaucratic state practices), with liberal political philosophies, and with a range of contending philosophies and ideologies that have arisen in reaction to liberalism. It is also associated with a distinctively modern kind of self (the individual); with capitalism as a global system of production, distribution, and consumption; and, crucially, with a particular style of knowledge production identified most closely with natural science. Among the other characteristic features of this distinctive complex cultural formation are rapid and continuous technological transformations, especially in connection with communication, transportation, economic production, consumption, and warfare.

An enormous amount of scholarship and polemics has been produced over the decades on the topic of "modernization" (Deutsch et al. 2002; Latham 2000). In much of the twentieth century, and continuing in the present century, the focus has been on the processes of *modernization* and related notions such as "development" understood as historical processes through which peoples and cultures of the formerly colonized lands, or what is commonly called "the Third World," might catch up with the industrialized (or "advanced") West. Modernization thus conceived has had enormous consequences implicating territoriality. At the most general level, these have included the proliferation and dispersal of the territorial nation-state as the sole legitimate expression of political identity and authority. Relatedly, the liberalization of land tenure associated with the penetration of capitalist political-economic structures and the establishment of more or less private property regimes has *re*territorialized much of the world of everyday experience. From one commonly held perspective, in order for the pre-modern or a-modern world to become modern it had to become like the West. And this means, among other things, participating or acquiescing in the peculiarly modern forms of territorialization associated with sovereignty and property. This involved more than the establishment of sovereign spaces (first the colonial, then the post-colonial state) and market-friendly systems of land rights (enforced by the repressive organs of these states). No less significantly, it entailed the emergence of social territorializations conducive to the emergence of a peculiarly "modern" sort of self that differs in important ways from the range of pre-modern selves that it has, with uneven success, supplanted. This is a (modern) self that is understood as being relatively unencumbered by communal or "tribal" affiliations (Giddens 1991; Taylor 1989). For example, one of the most significant episodes in the territorialization of race in connection with indigenous peoples of the United States was the policy of allotment (Greenwald 2002; Royster 1995). This was a program by which land that had been "set aside" for native peoples ("tribes") was broken up into discrete parcels and "allotted" to male-headed families. The surplus was then distributed to non-Indians. The stated purpose of this was to force native peoples to become modern individuals who would then adopt the mores and customs of the surrounding white community and more easily assimilate into the dominant culture. They would disappear as distinctive peoples. The stated expectation was that over time, as indigenous cultures withered, reservations – the territorial expressions of indigenous sovereignty – would be abolished (McDonnell 1991).

Again, speaking very generally, the idea of a modern self is a strongly individual or atomistic self that aspires to and thrives under conditions of freedom understood as minimally constrained choices. As conventionally understood, this liberal, modern self is a rights-bearing person whose life experiences are shaped less by "status" and more by "contract"; less by inherited hierarchies, more by choice. The relationship between territory and individualism (or the historic process of individuation) is by no means limited to the effects of private property. It is also manifest in the ways in which privacy, civil rights, civil liberties, and conceptions of human rights more generally are given spatial expression. In this regard consider the prima facie inviolability of the human body as the core territory of the modern self and the distress that commonly accompanies instances when this presumptive inviolability is overridden. Also, as I shall discuss below, an important implication for the invention of modern territoriality throughout the world is that the relatively modern self is a relatively mobile self.

Recently the theme of modernity has been engaged by those who, if not critical of the very idea of modernization, at least bring different dispositions and values to bear on the topic. Some writers may anticipate the arrival of an emancipatory post-modern epoch with enthusiasm. Some write more out of fear and dread of an imagined collapse of modernity and a repudiation of Enlightenment ideals that have allegedly fueled the progressive trajectory of modernity. This, by the very nature of how modernity is understood, would necessarily entail a regression to premodern darkness, chaos, and unfreedom. The theme of modernity is important to our larger purposes because the distinctive ideologies, discourses, practices, and processes associated with it (and the anti-modern currents it has engendered) have resulted in historically unprecedented transformations of human social life at the level of human experience for virtually every person alive on the planet today. Recognition of the historical contingency of modernity can open up important questions about the contingency of peculiarly modern forms and practices of territoriality.

One might usefully distinguish between the *territories of modernity* – or the enormous range of novel territorial forms through which modernity in all of its facets has found expression – and *modern territoriality*. Examples of territories of modernity include the high-tech prison cell, the refugee camp, the factory, the airport-gate waiting area, the trailer park, and countless others. *Modern territoriality* refers to the territorial processes and practices that arise out of the distinctive ways of thinking and acting in a modern world. Perhaps the clearest example of this is the capacity to conceive of the entire planet as a single place carved up into mutually exclusive, putatively sovereign states that constitute "the international." Modern territoriality reflects and reinforces the particular conceptions of self, society, identity, knowledge, and power and their often contradictory or indeterminate relationships. Emphasizing the distinctiveness of modernity and modern territoriality, predicated, as they are, on the continuous production of novelty, allows us to better understand the historicity of existing territorial configurations and those in the processes of becoming. (Indeed, only under conditions of modernity could one conceive of territories as "becoming.") Looking back we might trace these unfoldings on various scales of analysis. For example, global processes of "discovery," conquest, and colonization have played out very differently in different locations on the ground. The peoples and places of North America in the 17th century, Southeast Asia in the nineteenth century, and Amazonia in the 21st century were all subjected to the destructive force of European-centered or -derived colonialism and were territorialized in broadly similar ways. But the dissimilarities among these situations, in ideologies, technologies, global contexts, asymmetries of power, and forms of resistance, are also striking. "Modernity" is neither a one-size-fits-all nor a once-and-for-all phenomenon. How territoriality unfolds under various conditions is much more complex than a simple reference to modernity might suggest.

The edge of sovereignty: Canada (Quebec)–US (Vermont) border. Photo: Steven Silvern

The edge of jurisdiction: Massachusetts–New York state line. Photo: author

The edge of the local state: Sand Lake, New York. Photo: author

Conditions of entry: US Federal Arsenal, Watervliet, New York. Photo: author

"Never Mind the Dog": private residence, Santa Barbara, California. Photo: author

Territoriality in the workplace. Photo: author

Territory and mobility

Giving greater emphasis to the historical relationship between territory and modernity also highlights the dynamism of territorial configurations: their historicity and their propensity for continuous, if uneven, reconfiguration. Another closely related theme concerns the relationship between territory and diverse forms of mobility. That is, not only are territorial complexes themselves "in motion" so to speak, but much of how modern territories "work" (or function) is best seen in connection with motion across the lines that define territorial spaces. Even if the map of territories had remained unchanged for the last hundred years, the profound changes in communication, transportation, and state practices during that time have transformed the practical significance of boundaries, and therefore the territories themselves. The practices and processes of territoriality and territorialization have also changed dramatically. In this regard one might simply reflect on the history of passports and air travel (Torpey 2000). Territories are not simply static spatial classificatory containers. The life of territory is to be seen in the crossings-over, into and out of these meaningful spaces. This is most easily seen in connection with international boundaries either at the edges of states or in the dispersed "boundaries" associated with international air travel. In these places different categories of people-in-motion are sorted out according to territorial activities, status, or intentions. Immigrants, "guest workers," tourists, expatriate experts, humanitarian workers, diplomats, soldiers, smugglers, business people, deportees, refugees, touring musicians and athletes, and especially the millions of inhabitants of borderlands move back and forth across borders with (or without) the modern territorial documents of passports, visas, working papers, and birth certificates. It is in the context of this ceaseless motion that this form of territoriality is most active. In the examination of papers, the paying of bribes or duties, the seizure of contraband, the movement of troops, and the immobilization of aliens that territory becomes implicated into the fabric of lives.

And it is not only people in motion. The very idea of international "trade" (in contrast to domestic "exchange") presupposes the crossing of these lines. Commercial things, segmented commodity chains involving everything from missiles to happy-meal toys, from tropical hardwoods to roses, from heroin to antiquities, are in continuous cross-boundary circulation. The rapidly increasing circulation of people, things, capital, images, and ideas has given rise to claims about the increasing permeability of borders understood as the de-territorialization of the nation-state and the "erosion" of sovereignty (Cusimano 2000; Hudson 1999). I will examine these claims more fully in chapter 2. The point is that we can see contemporary territory more completely if we understand it more in terms of its relation to these movements and flows, and not simply as static boxes.

And this is not so only in the context of international territorializations. Modernity itself is commonly distinguished from other social formations by other, more generalized, forms of mobility, motion, and circulation. The intra-national, inter-urban mobilities associated with residential change, and the segmentation of work/home/consumption that requires most people in the United States, for example, to live their everyday lives divided among a number of political jurisdictions renders their relationship to territory very unlike that of those people whose lives take place within less complex, less fragmented territorial structures. The combination of social segmentation, territorial fragmentation, and technological transformation has facilitated the emergence of modes of "hyper-mobility" which have, in turn, resulted in fundamentally different relationships to territory. One may have the right to vote in only a small subset of the territorially defined units among which the moments of one's daily or weekly life is distributed. And perhaps these rights may not be in the territory that is most significant. Millions of Americans, for example, live and work in different states. Many municipalities have far more people who work or shop in them than live in them. At the same time, local territorially defined governments may have significantly diminished authority or control over what takes place within their boundaries. Rural towns or counties that are traversed by freeways may, at any given moment, have more people "in" them who have never heard of where they are than they have residents.

Territory and interpretation

As I discussed above, territoriality necessarily involves the assignment of meanings – of various sorts – to bounded spaces, to borders and boundaries, to the crossing of lines. These meanings may not be explicitly marked. They are often tacit or presupposed. One does not have to post a "Keep Out" sign on one's apartment door to have a reasonable expectation that strangers – or most familiars – will not enter uninvited. In interpersonal contexts the meanings of a territory (in the sense used by sociologists and environmental psychologists – see chapter 2) may be communicated orally, or perhaps by body positioning. However, the meanings associated with many forms of modern territory are often textually based nonetheless. Modern culture – literate culture, juridical culture – is very much a culture of "signage." As common experience will readily verify many of the non-commercial signs one encounters are markers of territory. The sign conveys an authority's commands about what we may, must, or must not do in the countless spaces that constitute our social-material environments:

> No Trespassing
> Tow-Away Zone
> Entering Mudville: Vendor's License Required
> School Zone: Use of Tobacco Products Prohibited
> No Shirt, No Shoes, No Service

and so on. Sometimes the consequences for disregarding the sign are also indicated ("$50 fine"). Sometimes the command carries with it a trace of its authorization ("Massachusetts General Laws, Chapter 266, section 120"). What could be clearer? "Keep Out" means keep out *or suffer unpleasant consequences.* "Authorized Personnel Only" puts you on notice that if you are not counted among the "authorized" you must not cross the threshold. The meanings and practical significance of "Whites Only" or "Entering the United States" certainly are not mysterious. If one of the posited functions of territory is that it clarifies and simplifies the social meanings of space, these examples seem to fit the bill.

Moreover, many of the meanings associated with modern territory refer back to other texts. Their quantum of meaning may be rooted in legal documents of various kinds, and these, in turn, may refer back still further to the rules by which the different legal texts are to be interpreted. Because they are *legal* texts they refer back to the state and its coercive capacities. The meanings of territory, or of particular territories, may derive from treaties, international agreements, constitutions, statutes, regulations, ordinances, contracts, deeds, work rules, and innumerable other texts. Any territory can potentially draw on these kinds of texts for a portion of its meanings. More accurately, the meanings of any given modern territory or territorial complex can be derived from a multitude of texts. In the mid-twentieth century it was very common for white property owners in the United States to create racial exclusionary zones by the use of private contracts. Participants would agree not to rent or sell their property to "Negroes" for a specified amount of time – commonly 25 or 50 years (Delaney 1998). These territories of exclusion (and expulsion) also gave each property owner "rights" with respect to the other properties in the territory. Dozens of legal cases arose challenging and defending these racialized spaces. Contending interpretations drew on prior cases, doctrines, constitutional provisions, and statements of policy to make legal sense of the territories. According to which among these competing interpretations prevailed (among white judges) the territories could be interpretively reinforced, modified, or erased. In the United

States, property law, environmental law, search and seizure law, Indian law, criminal law, the law of asylum, prison law, and so on are used to interpret territories countless times every day. Other nation-states have similar institutions and practices through which territories are subjected to interpretation. An apparently simple territory may be the spatial referent of an extremely complex set of textually based "meanings." Due to this complexity, even what appear to be the most obvious meanings may be open to divergent interpretations and reinterpretations. If territories convey meanings, these meanings have to be "read." More importantly, in many modern social contexts, the strategic reinterpretation or rereading of the meanings inscribed in territories may be a highly significant strategy for restructuring the workings of power. Earlier in this chapter I mentioned the case of U.S. *v.* Oliver, in which a majority of the United States Supreme Court reinterpreted a secluded area of private property as an "open field" for the purposes of authorizing warrantless searches by the police. The case can be understood as resulting from a struggle between "law and order" advocates and civil libertarians. As a result of the decision, the territoriality of privacy was diminished and the spatial scope of policing was augmented. The redistribution of power determined whether the property owner would or would not be incarcerated.

Reference to specifically legal texts and meanings connects the spaces in question to a particular institutionalized territorial form of power: that associated with the state. Many of the textualized territories of modern social life, from hemispheric free trade areas to state park camping grounds to tow-away zones, are created directly by state actors. Many others, such as those rooted in the prerogatives of private property, although created by putative "private" actors such as owners or managers, need to be authorized, validated, and enforced by state actors. Thus "No Trespassing" means much more than keep out. It carries with it the necessary implication that if one does not obey the message then the owner or manager may avail herself of access to state violence to enforce her claims of exclusiveness. Nearly all modern territories, one way or another, implicate complex relations of power that include, or can be reinterpreted to include at some point, those associated with the modern bureaucratic (local, sub-national, or national) state. And almost any territory occupies a position at the intersection of an open number of legal texts with reference to which it is made "meaningful." Nearly any modern territory, therefore, is interpretable, and, potentially, open to a range of divergent interpretations. Not all of these will be equally plausible or acceptable to the authorized interpreters. But this too is an issue that is contingent on the distribution of power.

Territory and verticality

One last dimension of territory that is infrequently given due attention but which allows us to see its complexity more clearly is "verticality." Territory is most commonly discussed in ways that treat it only "horizontally," that is, as a two-dimensional bounded space or mosaic of "like" spaces, such as those constituting the international system of states or patterns of local real-estate holdings or the territorialization of interior workplaces. Territory in these contexts refers to ways of marking mutually exclusive "insides" and "outsides" such as domestic/foreign, private/public, allowed/prohibited, ours/theirs, or mine/not mine. But, as the preceding discussion of the interpretability of territory suggests, in a modern social order characterized by the comprehensive global regimes of state sovereignty (as well as by systems of land tenure or property) every physical location – for example, where you are seated as you read these words – is positioned within a dense matrix of *multiple*, *overlapping* territories and territorial configurations. The "meanings" of each of these territories (and the power relations that these meanings imply) are established in relation to the other territories across the heterogenous "levels."

"Verticality" concerns the territorialized distribution of power among conceptually distinct entities with respect to some discrete segment of social space. Thus, discussions or debates about the scope or limits of national governments – most obviously, federal systems – and constituent states, provinces, or regions implicate the verticality of territories. So too do arguments about "local autonomy" vis-à-vis "higher" levels of government or other hierarchical organizations. Perhaps it is worth noting that talk of "verticality" and of "higher" and "lower" levels of territory is metaphorical. These are conventional ways of talking about relationships among territories (and the power relations that these imply) of heterogenous sorts. Regardless of the specifics of how various federalisms such as the United States and the European Community work, for example, there is nothing literally "higher" about these vis-à-vis the "lower" units of which they are composed. Something called "Canada" is not closer to the sun than something called "Prince Edward Island." The notion of verticality and the common discourses of "levels" do draw attention to (or perhaps "conjure up" would be a better term) the conceptual, metaphorical regulatory "boundaries" that separate and distinguish the discrete territories that are in seen in relation to them. And if the meaning and practical significance of a territory, whether a room, an apartment, an apartment complex, a municipality, a province, or a nation-state, is potentially open to divergent interpretations, and if the meanings of physically demarcated boundaries between different instances of the same kind of territory are debatable, then the multiple, figurative "lines" that separate different kinds of territories cannot be less so. And indeed, the politics of territoriality in these contexts may be as significant as the more commonly recognized politics of "horizontal" and homogenous territories. Debates about verticality commonly partake of the metaphors of "invasion" and "infringement" that are used in understanding "horizontal" territory.

As significant, at least in some places, is the conceptual boundary distinguishing sovereignty and property, or government and ownership, as these are thought to refer to distinct territorial regimes or spaces. Much of the law of real property in liberal legal orders is concerned with horizontal relations such as those involving adjacent landowners. But much is also centered on the relations structured by the territorialization of property rights and the territorialization of governments, local municipal, state or national, that property is embedded in. Again consider the case of U.S. *v.* Oliver in which the US Supreme Court validated a warrantless search of private property by the police. Looked at one way this can be seen as a reconfiguration of territoriality along a horizontal dimension. At issue there was whether locations relatively far from the owner's house should count as "private" (and therefore deserving of heightened protection provided by a warrant) or "public" regardless of ownership. But cases like this also implicate verticality insofar as they entail a diminishment of power (rights) associated with one sort of territory (property) and an augmentation of power (police authority) associated with a conceptually distinct but overlapping territory (the state). Moreover, this case was decided on the basis of an understanding of the relationship between state authority (in this case, the State of Kentucky) and Federal constitutional law (the Fourth Amendment as it has historically been interpreted to apply to state governments). The boundary between the territorialized regime of property and that of government is implicated in countless situations as diverse as housing codes, free speech, the regulation of sexuality, family law, and environmental protection. As we will see in chapter 4 in connection with the territorial genealogy of Israel/Palestine, the metaphorical boundary between "sovereignty" and "property" – and the politics of its inscription and revision – is among the most significant and active elements of territoriality more generally. The same point can be made with respect to many other contexts, such as the privatization or decollectivization of land in colonial or post-communist societies or deregulation in other countries. Whether power is conceptualized as being redistributed "downward" or "upward," the process is territorial insofar as the relevant participants are themselves territorialized. The verticality of territory is also at issue in those territorialized structures that embrace a multiplicity of nation-states. Trade areas, such as the North American Free Trade Area, territorially defined military co-ordination organizations such as the North Atlantic Treaty Organization, and the countless multilateral international regimes and organizations frequently give rise to arguments about the "erosion of sovereignty" of the constituent states. Any general discussion of territory that neglects verticality already closes off what may be among territory's most significant dimensions, insofar as any modern territory is embedded within complex constellations of distinct but mutually constitutive spaces through which power is distributed and redistributed. Once this is recognized, the simple and simplifying "ins" and "outs" of territory become much harder to accept.

Concluding Remarks

The aim of this chapter has been to open up the topic of territory by way of privileging aspects of territory – as a social, historical, cultural, political, and conceptual phenomenon – that are commonly marginalized or excluded altogether. As I have repeatedly said, territory is commonly understood as a device for simplifying and clarifying the operation of power in social relations. And no doubt it often does have this effect. "Keep Out" often does mean keep out. But a more productive task is to push beyond this cartoon vision to see what it might obscure. In the next chapter this aim is pursued in a somewhat different register through a survey of territory as it appears in various academic disciplines.

2

Disciplining and Undisciplining Territory

Introduction

Human territorial practices can be read back into the deep recesses of human time. Indeed, territoriality in various forms is commonly naturalized as a biological imperative (Ardley 1966), a primordial drive (Grosby 1995), and as essentially continuous with territoriality as exhibited by other primates and all animal species (Taylor 1988). And certainly, within the historical record of the West, fragments from Plato to Montesquieu can be identified to support the notion of an enduring core of what territoriality essentially is – and that it is, in some sense, essential (see, for example, selections in Kasperson and Minghi 1969). Nevertheless, the explicit theorization of territory and territoriality is a comparatively recent phenomenon that emerged under a specific set of (geo)political and historical conditions. Moreover, the recognition of territoriality as an essentially contested (non-essential) concept, a complex of ideas, images, and practices that are deeply problematic and deserving of theoretical scrutiny, is largely a development of the last 30 years.

The topic of territory has been a more or less central concern in a range of academic disciplines. For some, such as international relations and human geography, it has been quite significant. For others, such as anthropology, sociology, and psychology, it has been a more specialized interest of sub-fields such as political anthropology, urban sociology, and environmental psychology. For each discipline the meaning and significance of territory has been strongly conditioned by the specific preoccupations of the respective field of study, say, sovereignty (international relations), culture (anthropology), or privacy (psychology). Therefore, at first glance, the roles that territory plays in the various disciplinary discourses may appear to have little to do with one another. However, when looked at across a range of such discourses, various conceptions of territory are informed by a shared set of core presuppositions.

This chapter is in two parts. In the first part I present a survey of how territory has been treated in a set of disciplinary discourses. Given the large number of disciplines and the space constraints of this Short Introduction I do not pretend to present anything approaching a comprehensive survey. By necessity much is left out that no doubt ought to have been included, and what is included is given rather cursory treatment. The objectives are to bring out some of the principal contributions that each field has brought to our understanding of the topic and to explore the role that conceptions of territory play with respect to key concerns of these disciplines. I also note important gaps and disconnections that characterize these disciplinary approaches. Indeed, this part might best be seen as an exploration of *the academic territorialization of territory*, insofar as the different disciplines have conventionally used conceptions of territory both to delimit their more central concerns and to differentiate themselves from other disciplines.

In the second part I explore a set of interdisciplinary projects (Klein 1990) that explicitly repudiate this territorialization of territory and seek to illuminate some of what is obscured by more conventional disciplinary discourses. In fact, the case can be made that these interdisciplinary projects are themselves, in part, the products of reflection on territorial reconfigurations in the world such as those associated with globalization and post-colonialism.

Territory and its Disciplines

International relations

Clearly, the territorial state, the aggregate of states, and their associated boundaries which comprehensively cover the inhabited earth are among the most significant expressions of territoriality in the modern world. In many ways this spatial matrix informs or is the focus of attention of most social disciplines (Agnew 1993). Conventionally regarded as a quasi-natural "container" of its associated "society," the state "has acted like a vortex sucking in social relations to mould them through its territoriality" (Taylor 1994, 152).

Among the disciplines for which territory is a core concern is international relations (IR). But even here, as Ruggie claims, "It is truly astonishing that the concept of territoriality has been so little studied by students of international politics; its neglect is akin to never looking at the ground one is walking on" (1993, 174). This is to say that, while territory *is* a core concern for IR, *what* territoriality is and *how* it works are usually simply assumed and not explored – critically or otherwise. Territory demarcates the crucially constitutive "inside" and "outside" of states. It serves to differentiate the domestic from the foreign, the national from the international. But these distinctions in turn serve to support the identity of IR vis-à-vis political science. As Agnew has written, "It has been the geographical division of the world into mutually exclusive territorial states that has served to define the field of study" (Agnew and Corbridge 1995, 78). The often-stated idea is that "politics," strictly speaking, can only occur *within* a territorially defined political community. The various "relations" among sovereigns (between spaces) is not accurately describable as "politics" but as statecraft. Simply put, "the order within state borders is for others to study" (Agnew and Corbridge 1995, 81). This is simply to underline that a particular conception of territory is both a central object of disciplinary attention and constitutive of IR as an autonomous discipline.

The territorial state and the globally comprehensive "system" of states is a comparatively recent development in the world. Though there were antecedents, the modern territorial state system emerged in early modern Europe as a partial pragmatic solution to a number of local, historically contingent problems associated with the long-term transition from feudalism to capitalism. Territoriality as a spatial expression of the idea of exclusive sovereignty was formalized in a number of treaties such as the Treaty of Westphalia (1648) and the Treaty of Utrecht (1703) (Krasner 2001; Teschc 2003). But it took 300 years – and then some – to become *the* spatial organizing device on a planetary scale. Part of how the world-historical processes of imperialism, colonialism, decolonization and nationalist liberation can be understood is as the gradual and selective imposition of territorialized state structures onto non-European peoples and the resistance, accommodation, or selective acceptance of these by nationalized successors. In any case, it is important to remember that the sovereign territorial state has been a global phenomenon for less than 60 years.

Territory in this system of thought is tightly bound to the notion of "sovereignty" as a particular form of power (Krasner 1999; Walker and Mendlovitz 1990). Indeed, modern sovereignty is inextricable from modern territory. Formally, to be "sovereign" is to have absolute authority within a territorial space and to suffer no interference by parties outside of that space. The boundaries of the space demarcate the limits of authority. Any such interference is understood to threaten the integrity and therefore continued existence of the state. Therefore, interference or invasion is understood to trigger the exercise of the right of defense by any means necessary. *Formally*, the notion of territorial sovereignty entails equality among self-recognized sovereigns such as Uzbekistan, the Seychelles, Mexico, and the United States. *Practically*, of course, there exists a historically shifting and regionally diverse hierarchy of states that complicates this formal equality (Clark 1989).

IR has conventionally made a number of assumptions about territory and its relationship to sovereignty. But, principally, IR takes as given that "the modern form of territoriality . . . is based on linear, fixed boundaries separating continuous and mutually exclusive spaces" (Ruggie 1993, 168). These boundaries are understood as marking clear, unambiguous distinctions between interiors and exteriors, domestic relations and foreign, citizen and alien. And these, of course, are among the most significant categories of modern social life. The clarity and simplicity of territory and boundary underwrites the clarity and certainty of sovereign power. But IR theory also understands these in rather special ways. And, in a sense, working out the implications that are imagined to follow from this basic "spatial ontology", as Agnew (1998) puts it, is what IR theory is all about.

In the discourse of IR theory the boundary of the state has another, deeper meaning. It not only marks the outer limits of legitimate authority or the points along a line at which adjoining sovereigns come in contact, but also marks the utter distinction of "community" and "anarchy." Anarchy here is a term of art that, in its most basic usage, simply refers to the *absence* of sovereignty. But if "sovereignty" connotes "a homogenous and well bounded order of politics" (Ashley 1988, 238) and if "the sphere of domestic politics . . . is the sphere in which community is most fully realized" (Ashley 1987, 412), then "Anarchy, by contrast, betokens a field of equivocity and indeterminacy . . . a field of hazards, and perils that might put the pure presence of the sovereign in jeopardy" (Ashley 1988, 238). IR theory, then, not only assumes a particular conception of territory (as clear, closed, and fixed) but also tends to render territory in strongly dichotomous terms by way of mapping order/chaos, identity/difference, presence/absence, politics/power, and so on onto the lines and spaces through which global social life becomes intelligible.

But this characterization simplifies the territorial vision of IR theory too severely. This view applies more easily to some theoretical positions than to others. Criticisms and defenses of this position have actually animated what historians of the discipline call "the great debate" between "realists" and "idealists" (Maghroori 1982; Smith 1995; Walker 1989). "Realism" is a mode of thinking about "the international" in which sovereign states are the only relevant actors (Brown 1992; Buzan 1996). The principal preoccupations of realist international relations and associated discourses of foreign affairs and foreign policy are power, security, and order. Other imaginable themes of relationships among states, such as justice or ethics, are more or less irrelevant. Again, ideas such as "politics" or "community" which might conceivably form the basis for planetary justice and ethics are believed to be largely absent from relationships *among* states. This is what "anarchy" means.

In contrast, "idealism" – or, as this position is sometimes called, "liberalism," "pluralism," or "utopianism" – affirms the possibility of an "international community" of states in the absence of sovereignty (Little 1996). For thinkers in this vein there exists at least the possibility that international relations can be informed by (something like) universal moral commitments and a universal conception of justice. Chris Brown (1992) labels the distinction as one between "communitarians" (realists) and "cosmopolitans" (idealists). Practically, a cosmopolitan normative world order may be achievable through the establishment and invigoration of international organizations such as the League of Nations or the United Nations and through the proliferation and strengthening of "international regimes" or multilateral agreements such as those concerning human rights, the environment, and the non-proliferation of nuclear weapons (Hasenclever et al. 1997; Krasner 1983). Idealists, of course, recognize and affirm the fundamental significance of territorial sovereignty. But the positing of an "international community" expands the topics of discussion to include co-operation and the occasional imperative of humanitarian "intervention" in the domestic affairs of member states. Stronger versions of this position may call for practical limits on territorial sovereignty or the relocation of some attributes of sovereignty in a global polity. Even stronger versions are put forth by advocates of a world-wide, federated government (Glossop 1993).

For our purposes these debates within IR (and conventional foreign affairs discourse more generally) are structured by divergent conceptions of territory. Realists view the global territorial system as composed of mutually exclusive, spatially defined sovereigns organized on a flat two-dimensional mapping of power. Idealists imagine a territorialization of world power that is, by degrees, layered. Here, sovereign territories are constitutive components of a global community of states – a sort of mega-territory. As will become clearer as the present survey progresses, these two visions of territory have much more in common than the phrase "great debate" might suggest.

Human geography

Another discipline for which territory has been a traditional core concern is human geography. This field has historically distinguished itself from others by its focal interest in the social categories of place, space, and landscape. Territory, of course, is a significant element of human social spatial relations. These themes have also provided the foundation for conceiving of geography as a "synthetic" discipline, a sort of proto-interdisciplinary discipline whose function is to synthesize the knowledge produced in other fields and examine their interrelations in the material world (James 1972; Livingstone 1993). On the other hand, a rather pronounced form of disciplinarity has often been reconstituted through the proliferation of sub-fields such as political, economic, cultural, social, and urban geographies that often fall far short of the desired synthesis.

If IR can be characterized as a discipline for which territory is both foundational and yet rarely explicitly examined the same cannot be said for geography – or, at least, not in the same sense. Geographers over the generations have produced a large amount of knowledge about the forms, functions, and processes associated with territoriality and boundaries. I will be examining these below. But first I will mention two general features of the treatment of territory in geography that differ from its treatment in IR. First, while the bulk of the historic exploration of territory has focused on its connection with the nation-state, in the mid-twentieth century some geographers began to study the workings of territory *inside the state* in contexts such as federalism, intra-state boundary formation, municipal annexation, political redistricting, and so on (Dikshit 1975; Morrill 1981). Second, there is also a tradition in social geography of examining the workings of territory in *non-state* contexts. Here, the topic shades off into that of social space more generally (Ley 1983).

Genealogically, the treatment of territory in geography has been very close to that of realist IR. A central concern was with "geopolitics." As Saul Cohen defines it, "geopolitics is the applied study of the relationship of geographical space to politics" (1994, 17). In canonical and contemporary histories of political geography Friedrich Ratzel (1844–1904) is commonly identified as one of its "founding fathers" (Parker 1998). During the height of European imperial expansion he articulated a vision of territory that may strike contemporary observers as bizarre. Nonetheless, these understandings were important then and have a persistence and serviceability in the twenty-first century, despite the fact that, in many ways, his world and ours are radically different. But, perhaps, their enduring serviceability may be precisely in their utility for *denying* these differences and affirming the enduring vision presupposed by realist IR and the discourse of Great Power statecraft.

Friedrich Ratzel, an itinerant journalist turned academic geographer, gave expression to what has been called an "organicist" conception of state territory (Heffernan 2000; Ó Tuathail 1996). In his piece "The Laws of the Spatial Growth of States" (1896[1969]) he asserted, "in the state we are dealing with an organic nature. And nothing contradicts the nature of the organic than does rigid circumscription" (1896[1969], 17). "For political geography," he wrote, "each people located on its essentially fixed area, represents a living body which has extended itself over a part of the earth and has differentiated itself either from other bodies which have similarly expanded boundaries or by empty space" (p. 18). The organism here is not only an institution – the state – but its associated "people": a "culture" or "nation." Ratzel had what we might call a dermal theory of boundaries. "The boundary is the peripheral organ of the state, the bearer of its growth as well as its fortification, and takes part in all of the transformations of the organism of the state" (p. 23). Because the state is an organism there exists an almost biological imperative toward "growth" which is both literal and metaphorical. Territorial expansion is understood in terms of a stage theory of civilizational maturation. Law number one of "The Laws of Spatial Growth" states that "the size of the state grows with its culture" (p. 18). But what can it mean to talk about the *size* of a culture? Ratzel here is relying on a developmentalist notion of history or anthropology in which "lower" or "primitive" cultures may (or may not) evolve into more or less "advanced" or "mature" ones. By metaphorical extension a more mature culture is larger than a less mature one and so requires and deserves more space. Some of the latter progress to the status of "civilizations". "[T]he further we descend in the levels of civilization," he said, "the smaller the states become" (p. 19). These pseudo-Darwinian naturalizing imperatives gave a rhetorical appearance of scienticity to political geographical discourse in the early twentieth century. And, as one geographer has recently argued, "More than anything else Fredrick Ratzel provided a political vocabulary with an aura of science for the German Right, a vocabulary that articulated and justified an extreme nationalist desire for space that was to precipitate two world wars in the twentieth century" (Ó Tuathail 1996, 38).

We can see some of the influence of Ratzel's ideas in the work of Samuel Van Valkenburg's American text *Elements of Political Geography* (1940). Van Valkenburg used an explicitly organic, developmentalist model to arrange "nations" along a scale from "youthful" through "adolescence," "maturity," and "old age." Writing in 1939, he found only three "mature" states: the United States, the British empire, and France. Germany, Italy, and Japan, by contrast, were adolescents and were characterized by "their dynamic nature" (p. 9). Given the nature of adolescents, though, they "have to be kept in check in the hopes that maturity will soften their political views" (pp. 9–10). An important aspect of any nation, in Van Valkenburg's view, is its racial composition, race here "used in a biological sense" (p. 233). In a remarkable passage in which he sought "a better understanding of the reasons for the anti-Jewish outbreak" (p. 242) in the adolescent Third Reich, he made note of the prominence of Jews in the professions and the relative value of Jewish economic holdings in proportion to their numbers. "Here is the real reason for the trouble":

> One may call it racial antagonism based on the fact that Jews have characteristics not always attractive to others. One may call it economic jealousy based on the fact that Jews have ability to dominate certain fields... In the case of Germany, it was more the way in which the problem was handled than the problem itself that provoked the rest of the world. Germany certainly could have been more tactful. (1940, 243)

This is as good an illustration as can be imagined of Kearns's observation that "the geopolitical vision is never innocent. It is always a wish posing as analysis" (2003, 173).

As a direct result of this sort of thinking there arose in mid-century political geography a perceived difficulty. This was how to *de*politicize scholarship about politics and space so as to achieve something more nearly resembling "objectivity" or something worthy of the honorific "science." Among the most influential of the reformers was Richard Hartshorne. Writing "The Functional Approach in Political Geography" (1950[1969]) in the wake of World War II, Hartshorne sought to provide a disinterested analysis of territory, or, as he termed it, "politically organized area."

The task of the state, he argued, is to "establish complete and exclusive control over internal political relations – in simple terms, the creation and maintenance of law and order," and, in furtherance of this, "to secure the supreme loyalty of the people in all its regions, in competition with any local or provincial loyalties, and in definite opposition to any outside state-unit" (1950[1969], 35). He asserted that "the primary and continuing problem of any state is how to bind together more or less separate and diverse areas into an effective whole" (p. 35). The problem for the political geographer is to assess the relative strengths of "centripetal" (p. 38) and "centrifugal" (p. 36) forces acting within and on a given territorial state. This entails an analysis of relations of parts to whole and of the whole to the outside. This may be done through a study of existing territories and through examination of proposed territories in order to predict functional effectiveness. While Hartshorne had a more social and less naturalistic conception of the state, he did substitute biological metaphors with metaphors from physics.

Among the centrifugal forces Hartshorne mentioned were physical features such as mountain ranges, distance, the presence of "a different people, especially an unfriendly people" (p. 36), and regionally expressed diversity of language, religion, or economic activity. These, especially in combination, can potentially strain territorial integrity. The most significant of the centripetal forces that might counter these is what Hartshorne called "the state idea" (p. 38), or the state's reason for existing. Presumably a "state idea" exists in the minds of those who seek to create or maintain it. But there is no general universal state idea. Rather, a given state idea can only be discovered through particularized investigation. Investigation goes to answering questions such as: "Why is there Venezuela?", "Why is there Lebanon?", "What state idea binds together the various parts of Afghanistan?". One might then ask whether a given state's "state idea" is sufficiently forceful to counteract the centrifugal forces that would pull it apart territorially, or whether a more localized counter-state idea could be strong enough to support secession or partition. Interestingly, given recent events, his example of a state idea concerns Iraq whose "raison d'être" was rooted in

> (1) the recognition by the Great Powers of the special strategic and economic significance of the Mesopotamian region, and (2) the need to provide a pied à terre for Arab nationalism banished from Syria. On the basis of these two considerations there was established [note the passive voice] a territory embracing the settled Arab region of the Tigris–Euphrates plain, together with adjacent but dissimilar regions of mountain and desert tribes, the whole to be developed as a separate Arab state. (1950[1969], 40)

Rather presciently he added, "One would need to determine whether the Iraqis have since evolved a truly native concept" (p. 40).

Other mid-century geographers engaged in "boundary studies." Case studies were produced concerning boundary disputes, boundary changes, and other territorial revisions such as annexation and partition. In addition, though a decidedly minor theme, some geographers began to analyze "internal" boundaries such as those involving states of the United States, metropolitan areas, and local governments as well as the processes associated with political redistricting. These were usually not, however, theorized in terms of territory.

Before the 1970s territory as treated by human geographers was almost exclusively the domain of political geographers who were, in turn, almost exclusively concerned with the nation-state. As late as 1973, the eminent geographer Jean Gottmann could write a book entitled *The Significance of Territory* that was almost exclusively concerned with the history of statist territory in western Europe, and which attempted to account for its evolution in terms of tensions between "security versus opportunity" and "liberty versus equality." But by then, as we will see later in this chapter, the discipline of human geography had begun to change.

Anthropology

Unlike IR and political geography, territory has not been so central a theme in traditional anthropology. It has, however, been studied as an aspect of core topics such as culture and cultural change, inter-ethnic relations, kinship and lineage, symbolic meaning systems, resource use and land tenure, and pre- or non-state political organization. For us it is significant as a source of understandings of territory in contexts other than those centered on the sovereign state and, by virtue of that, as a source for more recent retheorizations.

Fredrik Barth's influential collection, *Ethnic Groups and Boundaries: The Social Organization of Cultural Difference*, explicitly focused on the dynamics of ethnographic boundary-making and maintenance. Barth noted: "Practically all anthropological reasoning rests on the premise that cultural variation is discontinuous... The differences between cultures, and their historic boundaries and connections, have been given much attention; the constitution of ethnic groups, and the nature of the boundaries between them, have not been correspondingly investigated" (Barth 1969, 9). These bounded cultural spaces differ in important ways from territory as treated in IR and geography. The focus in anthropology is more on isolation and diversity than on exclusion and exclusivity; more on self-ascribed identity and membership than on the exercise of power. The boundaries and the practices of boundary maintenance and negotiation involve issues of sameness and difference. "The critical focus," according to Barth, should be on "the ethnic *boundary* that defines the group, not the cultural stuff it encloses" (p. 15). The spaces defined by these boundaries may or may not have fixed material expression. In fact, they may move as "the cultural stuff" moves. From a perspective which assumes the spatial fixity of territory such boundary practices would by definition be non-territorial. Or perhaps "boundary" and "territory" are being used in their more metaphorical senses. From another perspective, however, one in which mobility and territory are not necessarily in opposition, the possibility arises of thinking about territory in ways that depart more dramatically from the IR prototype. For example, some anthropologists have examined the workings of territory and territoriality among hunter-gatherers, pastoralists, and nomadic peoples. This may initially seem puzzling insofar as these kinds of communities may be understood as *non*-territorial by definition in comparison with sedentary peoples. But again, the puzzle may be more a consequence of an overly simplistic or state-centric conception of territory.

The contributors to an important edited volume by Michael Casimir and Aparna Rao, *Mobility and Territoriality: Social and Spatial Boundaries among Foragers, Fishers, Pastoralists and Peripatetics* (1992), examine precisely this question. For example, this is how Alan Barnard describes territoriality among southern African hunter-gatherers:

> The social boundaries maintained in Bushman, or southern African hunter-gatherer society are defined according to language, culture and kinship relations. These boundaries include those between Bushmen and non-Bushmen, between one Bushman group and another, and within particular Bushman societies, between specific band clusters (nexuses), bands and households. The spatial boundaries to some extent run parallel to these, but they are not always identical. They depend on rights of access to territory and notions of the use of space in relation to appropriate modes of behavior. Some aspects of social and spatial boundary maintenance are unique to particular Bushman peoples, while others are common to all Bushmen or to hunter-gatherers in general . . . Given that territoriality exists in the context of a wider set of relations between man and environment and between individuals, any examination of territoriality among hunter-gatherers must account for its significance within this larger set of relations. (1992, 137–138)

We might also note that an ethnographic sensibility gives greater prominence to the empirical details of life-worlds than is commonly found in general theories of "the state." Another contributor to this collection, Andrzej Migra, discusses some of the specific workings of territoriality among the Roma of eastern Europe:

> A particular form of territoriality connected with the basic socioeconomic unit of peripatetic "Gypsies," known in the Polish context as *tabor* . . . The notion of territory did not correspond here to a single geographical or administrative area, but rather to a set of spaces within which a given tabor . . . was or could be physically present at any given moment; it was conjured up whenever its members happened to be located and was thus a kind of shifting or mobile zone . . . Its basis was the right of priority, respected by other *tabors*, and the existence of a feeling of being "temporary proprietors," since it was partially negotiated with local authorities. (Migra, in Casimir and Rao 1992, 268)

At an even finer grain of analysis Joseph Berland discusses the "peripatetic territories" of traveling peoples of Pakistan. "Across all peripatetic communities of Pakistan," he writes,

> the basic social unit is the tent (*puki*) where *puki* specifies an actual physical structure with definite spatial boundaries; it also includes the broader

cultural notion of the primary social unit comprised of a female, her spouse, and resident offspring...wherever situated, both internal and immediate external space is considered the exclusive domain or territory of its members....Two or more tents traveling together...form a *dera*. *Dera* are only corporate to the extent that members cooperate toward maintaining spatial boundaries around camp sites, promote harmony, and pool knowledge and experience about local markets...(Berland 1992, 383–384, 386)

Sometimes a number of *dera* may concentrate in a locale to form a temporary camp:

In the open spaces available each *dera* will maintain the maximum distance possible from each other...[E]ach camp has a perimeter and defined space separating one *dera* from another. To the outsider this is difficult to see; however, *dera* members and especially tent dogs, establish and carefully defend boundaries as regions about half-way between each camp area. (1992, 388–389)

Clearly the vision of territory used by these anthropologists contains many of the elements of other visions we have surveyed. They are bounded spaces defined by and defining aspects of identity and difference that condition differential access and involve defense or the dynamics of power and authority. But equally clear are the ways in which these territories differ from conventional understandings that take the formally sovereign state as the prototype. These territories are rather ephemeral and, indeed, they can move.

Perhaps a more familiar form of territory studied by anthropologists is that associated with indigenous systems of land tenure and customary law among non-Western peoples. Land tenure, including liberal property systems in the West, necessarily involves the territorialization of what translates, albeit uneasily, into "rights." Speaking of the Wola of Papua New Guinea, Paul Sillitoe writes, "Land rights concern boundaries...and the problem of territorial definition...Rights to land are one of the principal arenas in which people express and act their kinship and identity relations with kin-defined obligations controlling access" (1999, 333). Ethnographic investigations of land tenure bring home to the West a recognition of an immense variety of ways of imagining and practicing territory beyond those presupposed by IR and political geography. The rules, images, and practices of customary land tenure – regarded as elements of indigenous territoriality – are inextricable from ways of life and ways of acting in social, symbolic, and material worlds. Anthropological approaches to land tenure also move our survey further from state-centered conceptions and open up a wider variety of senses of the political. Also important are ethnographic studies of the local politics of land with respect to access, use, allocation, or transfer of rights to particular spaces and the dynamics of territorial disputes (Benda-Beckmann 1979; Moore 1986), studies concerning conflicts between customary land law and colonial or post-colonial state law (Benda-Beckmann 1999; Tocancipá-Falla 2000–01), and the territorial reconfigurations associated with processes of land reform, collectivization and decollectivization, and the penetration of multinational corporations and statist development projects in indigenous areas (Strathern and Stewart 1998; Yetman and Búrquez 1998).

In comparison with IR and geography, anthropological discourse moves conceptions of territory in three directions. First, by shifting the focus from the West to "the rest" – into the spaces of empire and the colonies – it presents a wider variety of human territorial practices and processes. Second, by examining "customary" practices it moves us further away from the state as the only expression of territory even as it directs attention to the relation between statist and non-statist forms. Third, by way of detailed ethnographic studies it presents fine-grained analyses of the workings of territoriality within villages, fields, gardens, and paths in ways that implicate the involvement of territory with the unfolding of human lives.

Sociology

Part of the distinctiveness of the discipline of sociology vis-à-vis anthropology has conventionally turned on taken-for-granted conceptions of space and territory (here/there, home/field, West/the rest, metropole/colony) and, by extension, taken-for-granted notions of identity. Sociologists, by convention, study the modern societies to which they belong. In many ways, though, conceptions of territory in sociological discourse are analogous to those in anthropology – albeit with significant modifications derived from the features that are understood as marking the distinctiveness of modernity: for example, individuation and the relationship between the individual and society, urbanization, stratification, and deviance. One parallel theme is the constitutive effects of boundaries. Anthony Cohen's 1985 work on social boundaries, for example, is similar, in broad outline, to Fredrik Barth's. "The consciousness of community", he writes, "is ... encapsulated in perception of its boundaries, boundaries which are themselves largely constituted by people in interaction" (1969, 13). Discussions of territory are especially prevalent in sociological treatments of urban street gangs and their "turfs." As sociologists Decker and Van Winkle argue, "the threat of a gang in a geographically proximate neighborhood [turf] serves to increase the solidarity of the gang, compels more young men to join their neighborhood gang and enables them to engage in acts of violence that they may not otherwise have committed" (Decker and Van Winkle 1996, 22). Another sociologist, Felix Padilla, discusses the expectation of violent defense of territory among the gangs he studied, and

> the matter-of-factness associated with acts of violence used to protect turf. Almost all gang members accept it as a given that incursions on their turf will be met with violent responses, as will their trespasses onto the turf of rival gang members. Talk of the need for defending gang turf occurs on a regular basis among gang members, far more often than do actual acts of defense. In this way the atmosphere of symbolic vigilance against the threat of outside intruders draws the gang together and prepares it to use the expressive (and excessive) violence often associated with defending home territory against rival gangs. (1992, 114)

One attempt to craft a specifically sociological conception of territory that focused on the fine grained micro-territoriality of social life was Lyman's and Scott's "Territoriality: A Neglected Sociological Dimension", published in the journal *Social Problems* in 1967. In this piece the authors constructed a typology of territories characterizing modern, urban America. Among its constituent types were: "**public territories**," "those areas where the individual has freedom of access, but not necessarily of action, by virtue of his claim to citizenship" (1967, 237). However, this freedom of access is a function of social identity, such that some people are not fully members of "the public." "[C]ertain categories of persons are accorded only limited access to and restricted activity in public places" (p. 238). For example, "Negroes will not be found leisurely strolling on the sidewalks of white neighborhoods, though they might be found laying the sewer pipe under the streets." Then there are "**home territories**," in which "the regular participants have a relative freedom of behavior and a sense of intimacy and control over the area. Examples include, makeshift clubhouses of children, hobo jungles, and homosexual bars." The authors noted that, in these last-mentioned territories, "The style of dress and language among patrons at a bar may immediately communicate to a homosexual that he has arrived in home territory" (p. 240). This suggests that territoriality has a performative or semiotic aspect.

Focusing on territory at a still more intimate scale Lyman and Scott observed that, "Surrounding any interaction is an invisible boundary, a kind of social membrane." Such boundaries enclose "**interactional territories**." These are "characteristically mobile and fragile." Finally, there are "**body territories**, which includes the space encompassed by the human body and the anatomical space of the body." Implicated in body territories are "the rights to view and touch the body." "[S]exual access to the female," they write, "is deemed the exclusive right of the husband so long as he exercises propriety with respect to his status" (p. 241). Implicit in their description is a pronounced asymmetry of rights and power. Use of the passive voice ("is deemed") is strikingly at odds with what is being described. One might also ask what sort of boundary practices are invoked by the phrase "exercises propriety." The body territory of "the female" is thus the "home territory" of "the husband." "A person who persists in violating the extraterritorial space of another of the same sex may be accused of tactlessness and suspected of homosexuality, while uninvited intersex invasions may indicate unwarranted familiarity" (p. 241). Lyman and Scott also discuss forms of encroachment – violation, invasion, and contamination – and modes of reaction. Of historical interest is their notion of "**free territory**":

> Free territory is carved out of space and affords opportunities for idiosyncrasy and identity . . . [O]pportunities for freedom of action . . . are intimately connected with the ability to attach boundaries to space and command access to or exclusion from territories . . . In American society where territorial encroachment affects nearly all members of society, certain segments of the population are particularly deprived, namely, Negroes, women, youth and inmates of various kinds. (Lyman and Scott 1967, 248)

One response to the absence of free territory or the violation of home territory is what the authors call "penetration," by which they mean "the exploitation and modification of inner space in the search for free territory." For example, "contemporary college youth sometimes partake of hallucinogenic and psychedelic drugs in order to make an inner migration (or "take a trip" as the popular idiom has it)" (p. 241).

A similar approach may be seen in the work of the eminent sociologist Erving Goffman, whose 1971 book, *Relations in Public: Microstudies of the Public Order*, contains a chapter on "Territories of the Self." A territory, for Goffman, is best understood as a "preserve" or "a field of things." "The boundaries of this field are ordinarily patrolled and defended by the claimant" (1971, 29). Like Lyman and Scott, Goffman presents a typology of territories that are of sociological interest. Among the territories that give structure to the micro-politics of modern American society are:

- **Personal Space**. "The space surrounding an individual, anywhere within which an entering other causes the individual to feel encroached upon, leading him to show displeasure and sometimes to withdraw" (1971, 29);

- **The Stall**. "The well bounded space to which individuals can lay temporary claim, possession being on an all-or-none basis...They provide external, easily visible, defendable boundaries for a spatial claim" (1971, 32–33); and
- **The Sheath**. "The skin that covers the body, and, a little remove, the clothes that cover the skin...the purest kind of egocentric territoriality" (1971, 38).

Goffman also discussed modes of marking territories, modalities of violation, and offenses.

These sociological conceptions of territory are similar to anthropological ones insofar as those who are behaving territorially are analogized to ethnic groups or sub-cultures. But the sociological vision, premised as it is on a form of individualism characteristic of modernity, focuses its attention on the territories of the self, especially as these are conditioned by the public/private distinction.

Psychology

The sub-disciplines of behavioral and environmental psychology also take the theme of territory quite seriously (Altman 1975; Brown 1987). Perhaps, following Lyman and Scott, they can be understood as charting the connections between territory as "inner space" and the territorialization of the external world. *Human Territorial Functioning*, by Ralph Taylor (1988), is one of the most detailed and substantial works on psychological territoriality. Explicitly situated within "an evolutionary framework" that regards human territoriality as continuous with non-human territoriality, Taylor discusses territory in terms of order, conflict reduction, experiential stress reduction, and the relative efficacy of various territories to perform these functions. After laying out a general model of territorial functioning in the first six chapters of the book he offers detailed analyses of territorial functioning in four generic settings, devoting a chapter to each. The **indoor residential setting** ("locations where the occupant or occupants can exercise some degree of excludability and control over activities," p. 141) examines such features as the effects of floor plans, furniture placement, and specific social relationships. For example, Taylor claims that "a greater degree of liking between individuals sharing the same interior residential setting should result in a more trouble-free territorial functioning. As liking increases there should be a more consensual spatial and temporal allocation of particular locations within the setting" (p. 147). The category **outdoor residential spaces**

close to home concerns the functional working of territory in backyards, alleys, and street blocks around the home. Important here are marking behaviors such as "swept sidewalks, scrubbed steps, trimmed lawns and bushes...pink flamingos, pottery cats...[and] seasonal decorations at Christmas, Easter, or Halloween" (p. 177). These territorial markers convey information to neighbors, passers-by, and would-be burglars. For example, the strategic placement of a lawn jockey might be interpreted as signifying: "He is a vigilant resident who is always on the lookout to be sure that people don't mess up his property. You can't get away with anything around his place" (p. 179). Territoriality might also function in these contexts to facilitate individuation, stress reduction and the strengthening of acquaintanceship ties or neighborliness. **Regular use settings** involve the functioning of territory in contexts such as workplaces, offices, and bars, while the category **minimal territorial functioning** appertains to more ephemeral territorial behaviors in places such as classrooms and beaches. Taylor applies his theory of territorial functioning to various social problems such as disorder, crime, and vandalism and finds that an increase in surveillance and territorial markers can decrease disorder.

The vision of territory given expression by environmental psychologists such as Taylor tends to universalize and naturalize the peculiar cultural practices and concerns of moderns – or, more specifically, middle-class Americans of the late twentieth century. As an elaborate representation of this local way of territorializing social life, it demonstrates the extent to which fear may be fundamental to the construction of these life-worlds.

Summary

In this brief and highly selective exploration of disciplinary discourses on territory and territoriality we have seen how territory is understood as being implicated in a wide range of social relations, from the interpersonal to the international, and how different forms and expressions of power are implicated in the constitution and maintenance of territories. Taken together these views reveal the complexity and significance of territory – or at least what various academic observers *call* territory. But, in fact, they are rarely "taken together." Each disciplinary discourse tends to slice through territory *as such* and subordinate it to the core concerns that distinguish the disciplines from one another. (An important exception to this is the work of Robert Sack, whose *Human Territoriality* will be examined at length in chapter 3.) Taken together one may be impressed most strongly by what is missing: how – if at all – they might

hang together. What we see is the disciplinary territorialization of territory which treats states, cities, ethnic groups, communities, gangs,
families, and individuals as if each inhabited its own separate world
that can only be examined in isolation. Perhaps the differences are strong-
est at the extremes. We began our survey with IR, which imagines
political territories without people, and ended it with environmental
psychology, which imagines personal territories without politics. Along
the way we have seen how the working sense of territory shifted from the
rather rigid, formal, enduring, and violent to more fluid, informal,
ephemeral, and even mobile forms. Perhaps the disciplinary discourses
can be understood as slicing the world up according to scale, and our
trajectory as having traced a path from the macro to the micro. But again,
the question of whether or how these scales articulate has been neglected.
Territory is itself "contained" by scale, and scale assigns the disciplines
their proper place in modern systems of knowledge production.

Nevertheless, this survey may also reveal important commonalities
among many of the different visions. And these commonalities have
become the subject of a significant degree of criticism of late. Among
the commonalities is a tendency to see territory in terms of rather sharp
either/or, inside/outside binary oppositions, with rather unified, homogenous "insides" and relatively clear boundaries. In each as well there is
a pronounced flatness, as "horizontal" differences and relations are
privileged over what in chapter 1 I called "vertical" differences and
relations. The disciplines stress territory in connection with, say, state/
state, group/group, or self/self relations and not with more heterogenous
and complex relations. That is, there is a strong tendency to read territory
as differentiation within disciplinary terms of sameness. There is also a
bias toward focusing on this or that territory or boundary in isolation, at
the expense of analyzing more complex territorial mosaics. Moreover,
there is the sense in which the extreme points of our survey are simply
versions of each other. IR sees the state as a sort of unified individual self
writ large, while psychology sees the self as a sort of sovereign state writ
small. For each, territoriality is tightly connected to ideas of self-determination and conceptualized in terms of fear, danger, security, invasion,
control, defense, violence, and the loss of integrity.

Deterritorializing the Disciplines

In the last third of the twentieth century scholars from various "home"
disciplines began to increasingly explore ways of escaping the territoriality of territory through a range of interdisciplinary projects. Drawing on
an expanded array of theoretical resources such as post-structuralism,

post-modernism, political economy, and feminism, these writers began to express a more explicit reflexivity regarding the production of knowledge and the ways in which established disciplinary perspectives both focus attention on some aspects of territoriality and limit the scope of inquiry. There has also been an increased awareness of the relationship between knowledge (representations of territory) and power. More skeptical of at least some of the claims advanced under the name of modernity, if not about the very idea of modernity, some of these projects evince as well a heightened sensitivity to the effects of conventional conceptions of territory. Indeed, the theme of territory has been so thoroughly engaged by so many scholars from within so many interdisciplinary projects that the present era can with some justification be regarded as a Golden Age of territoriality theory. In part, this is the result of a generational shift and an intensification of interdisciplinarity across the social sciences. In part, it is the result of perceived changes in the world that increasingly demonstrate the inadequacy of conventional understandings. It is also true that these newer approaches tend to be critical. They are critical of inherited disciplinary discourses, critical of the ways in which power is actually exercised and experienced vis-à-vis territoriality, and critical of the complicity of the former in the workings of the latter. The result of all of this ferment is the emergence of novel ways of understanding territory that have turned conventional conceptions inside out.

In this part of the survey we will examine some of the significant interdisciplinary projects in a way that more or less tracks the disciplinary discourses reviewed in the preceding sections. First I will discuss post-structuralist approaches to IR and the emergence of critical geopolitics in human geography. Then I will touch upon some key issues in radical and critical geography more generally as these relate to changed understandings of territory. This will be followed by a brief exploration of the role of culture theory, and more specifically, border theory in recent retheorizations. This section will conclude with a brief discussion of what may be the most intensely argued theme in current debates about territory: globalization and its alleged de-territorializing effects.

The newer international relations

The discipline of international relations has not been immune to the theoretical and practical shifts of the era. Influenced by social theories and methods that had not previously informed IR scholarship, many practitioners have attempted to break out of the box defined by the terms of "the Great Debate" among realists and idealists. As a first step they have subjected the terms of the debate to sustained analysis and critique. This has entailed a critical examination of the very ideas of "sovereignty," "anarchy," and "the international" as these are deployed in traditional IR discourse. Because these concepts are all made intelligible through unexamined notions of territoriality, it is not surprising that these critical explorations have resulted in the invention of novel and productive reconceptualizations of territory and its relationship to power, meaning and experience. Here I will just touch on three strands of the critique: historicization, discursivity, and a shift in focus from territories as static containers to the borders that define them and mobility of people who cross these borders.

To the extent that the discourse of IR statecraft and geopolitics assumes the territorial state as a quasi-natural, primordial spatialization of power, one of the principal tasks of critical IR theory is to assert the historicity of this formation. This means not simply tracing the emergence, "evolution," and global diffusion of the territorial state. Nor is inquiry limited to studying the changing configurations within an enduring framework, as in conventional political geography. Rather, critical IR theory emphasizes the historical, cultural, and political *contingency* of the framework itself. That is, it aims to denaturalize, and thereby to repoliticize, one of the most fundamental modern relationships between power and territory. R. J. B. Walker, a pioneer in this endeavor, writes,

> The modern principle of state sovereignty has emerged historically as the legal expression of the character and legitimacy of the state... Most fundamentally, it expresses the claim by states to exercise legitimate power within strictly delimited territorial boundaries. This claim now seems both natural and elegant... [C]laims about state sovereignty suggest permanence; a relatively unchanging territorial space to be occupied by a state characterized by temporal change; or a spatial-cum-institutional container to be filled by the cultural or ethnic aspirations of a people. Governments and regimes may come and go, but sovereign states... go on forever. (1993, 165–166)

In contrast to this Walker tells a different kind of story. "Once upon a time," he tells us,

> the world was not as it is. The patterns of inclusion and exclusion we now take for granted are historical innovations. The principle of state sovereignty is the classic expression of those patterns, an expression that encourages us to believe that either those patterns are permanent [realism] or that they must be erased in favor of some kind of global cosmopolis [idealism]. Its fixing of unity and diversity, or inside and outside, or space and time is

not natural. Nor is it inevitable. It is a crucial part of the practices of all
modern states, but they are not natural or inevitable either. (1993, 179)

If the territorialization of political power is described more in terms of
contingency than necessity, then new lines of inquiry are opened up that
might allow one to see further through territoriality.

A second and related critical task is to emphasize territory as the *effect*
of discursive practices (hence Walker's references to "claims" and "expressions") and to focus particular attention on the ways in which these
claims and assumptions work in the traditional discourses of IR, statecraft, foreign affairs, and, by extension, in the popular imagination
(George 1994). Discourse here does not simply refer to the transparent
communication of "meanings" about lines and spaces, or even to the
workings of rhetoric, but rather to the patterned, structured modes of
thinking, saying, writing, and doing that have the effect of essentializing
or universalizing sovereignty, sovereign territory, and their associated
images and oppositions. Against this, Walker offers

> a reading of modern theories of international relations as a discourse that
> systematically reifies an historically specific spatial ontology, a sharp
> delineation of here and there, a discourse that both expresses and con-
> stantly affirms the presence and absence of political life inside and outside
> the modern state as the only ground on which structural necessities can
> be understood and new realms of freedom and history can be revealed.
> (1993, ix)

Moreover, these conventional territorial discourses and their associated
knowledge claims, built as they are on expertise of a particular sort and
informed by inherited IR theories, are not inert with respect to the
practical workings of power. As Phillip Darby puts it, "international
relations as a system of thought... cannot be understood apart from the
hegemonic position of the West in global relations and especially the
historical preeminence of Britain and the United States" (2003, 149).
Most likely he means that it cannot *accurately* be understood, because it
certainly *is* understood, most usually apart from these political conditions. More bluntly still, Smith states, "in the name of enlightenment and
knowledge, international theory has tended to be a discourse accepting
of, and complicit in, the creation and recreation of international practices
that threaten, discipline and do violence to others" (1995, 3). Among the
most fundamental of the knowledge claims are those relating to territory.

Another prominent critical IR theorist, Richard Ashley, also examines
the "reigning interpretive dispositions" of traditional IR theory. In a
piece entitled "The Geopolitics of Geopolitical Space" (1987), he proposes
instead a "genealogical attitude" toward the dominant discourse of state

territorial sovereignty. This is a skeptical attitude toward the production and circulation of knowledge claims, which

> dispose[s] one to regard the "autonomy" and "identity" of the field as a consequence of the plays of power among plural elements. One is disposed to look for the strategies, techniques, and rituals of power by which multiple themes, concepts, narratives, and practices are excluded, silenced, dispersed, recombined, or given new or reversed emphasis, thereby to privilege some elements over others, impose boundaries, and discipline practice in a manner producing just this normalized division of practical space. (1987, 41)

This "space" simultaneously refers to the discursive constitution of "the field" of IR vis-à-vis political science, and to the representations of political territory that underwrite its posited "autonomy" and "identity," and which, indeed, are inseparable from it as a field of authoritative expertise. This spatial discourse is clearest, perhaps, with respect to the structural oppositions of inside/outside, according to which sovereignty/anarchy, domestic/foreign, and national/international are made intelligible.

The purpose of these critical exercises, again, is to demonstrate the *contingency* – the non-necessity – of modes of thinking, practices of theorizing, "ways of world-making" associated with modern, state-centered territoriality and territorialized identities. It is to stress that these are contingent on extant distributions of power and to provide an opening through which to imagine other possibilities, constellations of space–power–meaning–experience other than those which modern territorialities admit. Walker concludes his book *Inside/Outside* (1993) by asking us to imagine how it might be possible "to articulate a plausible account of identity, democracy, community, responsibility or security without assuming the presence of a territorial space, a sharp line between here and there" (p. 182).

Attention to the workings of a dichotomized inside/outside both in consciousness and in the ways in which modern, state-centered territorializations of power sustain other oppositions is part of a broader shift toward the critical analysis of borders. Borders may be looked at as other than the clear, stable edges of sovereign states. More specifically, in critical IR theory there is a shift away from viewing territories as sealed containers toward the exploration of trans-border mobilities. I will examine this theme in more detail below. For present purposes, recognition of trans-border mobilities is seen to require a reorientation of conventional IR thinking about territory. Peter Mandaville, for example, asserts that because of the increasing significance of what he terms "translocality" in global social life, "the very nature of political territoriality may be undergoing certain transformation" (1999, 653). Indeed, he argues that "territory in its classic sense – which I understand as a sphere delimited by the exclusive jurisdiction of a particular political hegemony – may no longer constitute the primary space of the political" (p. 654). "Borders," he writes, "have been rendered more permeable by non-corporeal expressions of political agency...and people live their lives across and between territories rather than within the "little boxes" of official state space" (p. 658). He advocates that IR theorists shift their attention to studying the "politics of translocality" which, he claims, could provide "a richer account of identity, community and territory" (p. 655). This "de-territorialization" thesis has not gone unanswered, as we will see below. The newer IR theories have subjected inherited understandings of territory to an unprecedented level of critical analysis. The common-sense world of sovereign nation-states and their associated identities and powers appears to be little more than the setting for a shell game played out on a planetary scale.

Critical geopolitics

A significant contribution to the general retheorization of state-centered territoriality is the project of critical geopolitics as developed chiefly by political geographers. According to key participants Simon Dalby and Gearóid Ó Tuathail, this is "an ongoing intellectual interrogation of the politics of geographical knowledge in both international and national politics and, increasingly, in those spaces that confound these distinctions" (1996, 452). Ó Tuathail writes that

> "Critical geopolitics" promises both a new degree of politicization to understandings of geography and a new degree of geographicalization to the study of global politics. It seeks to transgress the boundaries and challenge what are held to be essential identities, whether they be imagined communities or inherited philosophical boundaries. (1994, 525)

One primary objective is to critically analyze the very idea of "geopolitics" and its effects. For example, Ó Tuathail presents this fairly standard definition of "geopolitics" as given by political geographer Saul Cohen: "The essence of geopolitical analysis is the relation of international political power to the geographical setting" (Cohen 1973, 29). He then notes that packed into this simple definition are assumptions that

> geopolitics is a fixed point, a known identity, a presence. This point is located at the intersection of two separate domains or territories of

knowledge: "international political power" and "geographical setting." Where these lands overlap is the location of geopolitics . . . The associative relations of this term map a relationship between geography and its binary opposite (history/politics/ideology). Within the geopolitical tradition, geography is projected as natural not historical, passive, not dynamic, permanent, not transitory, solid, not fluid, a stage rather than a drama. (Ó Tuathail 1994, 531)

Critical geopoliticians also analyze and politically contextualize the writings of key figures in conventional geopolitics and political geography such as Ratzel and Hartshorne in order to demonstrate the complicity of knowledge producers and the legitimation of power (Bassin 2003; Heffernan 2000; Kearns 2003). Critical geopolitics aims to destabilize the taken-for-granted conceptions of territory that inform much of contemporary thinking about power at all scales of analysis and experience.

One important contributor to the rethinking of political space is geographer John Agnew. Drawing on IR scholars such as Walker and Ashley, Agnew presents an analysis of what he calls "The Territorial Trap" (1994, reprinted in Agnew and Corbridge 1995). This analytic trap consists of "the specific [and implicit] geographical assumptions that underpin the conventional representations" of political territory in IR and political geography (1995, 79). It also underwrites much of the unexamined common sense of most social disciplines.

> From this point of view states are unitary actors whose nature is determined by their interaction with one another. Each state pursues a calculus of status maximization relative to the others. No spatial unit other than the territory of the state is involved in international relations. Processes involving sub-state units (e.g. localities, regions) or larger units (e.g. world regions, the globe) are necessarily excluded. (1995, 81–82)

The first and "most fundamental" misconception is one in which "states have been reified as a set of fixed units of sovereign space. This has served to dehistoricize and decontextualize processes of state formation and disintegration. Realism and idealism have both relied heavily on this assumption" (Agnew and Corbridge 1995, 83–84). This part of the trap puts "security" – (mis)understood in a very specific way – at the very heart of geopolitical concern. "What is at stake is the survival and maintenance of the state over its territory. The total sovereignty of the state over its territorial space in a world fragmented into territorial states gives the state its most powerful justification. Without this the state would be just another organization" (p. 84). The second assumption concerns "the use of domestic/foreign and national/international polarities [that] has served to obscure the interaction between processes operating at different scales" (p. 84). Unquestioned reliance on these conceptual dichotomizations facilitates the denial of the verticality of territory. This, in turn, obscures the operation of forces and processes that are less amenable to a flat, horizontal reading of territorial power. The third principal misconception is one in which "the territorial state has been viewed as existing prior to and as a container of society. As a consequence society becomes a national phenomenon. This assumption is common to all types of international relations theory" (p. 84). When an analyst (or anyone else) makes these assumptions, she has fallen into the trap. This is not without the severest of consequences – especially concerning one's ability to assess contemporary events. For example, the territorial trap makes it much easier to view warfare as a violent encounter between, say, "the United States" and "Iraq," each of which is assumed to be an unproblematic unified entity. It thereby obscures the workings of, for example, global militarism, the economic control of oil, the role of international finance, religious fundamentalisms, and the high level of political dissent within each of these political spaces. Likewise, when migration across the US–Mexico border is viewed from the perspective of the trap, one "sees" conflicts between nation-states but fails to "see" the dynamics of race, class, and gender and the restructuring of the international division of labor that are, arguably, more significant.

But, Agnew argues,

> Each of these assumptions is problematic and increasingly so. Social, economic and political life cannot be ontologically contained within the territorial boundaries of states...Complex population movements, the growing mobility of capital, increased ecological interdependence, the expanding information economy and the "chronopolitics" of new military technologies challenge the geographical basis of conventional international relations theory. (Agnew and Corbridge 1995, 100)

Critical geopolitics is perhaps best understood as a component of critical geography more generally. In common with scholars in other social disciplines, geographers have been influenced by and have contributed to an expanding range of theoretical resources in the last generation such that the theoretical locations (and conversations within them) are often more significant than disciplinary locations (and conversations within them). For example, feminist geographers may be in fuller communication with feminists in other disciplines than they are with other geographers; post-modernist geographers may feel more kinship with other post-modernists than with other geographers. And while human geography is concerned with much more than territory, many of the theoretical developments have had a profound effect on how territory has come to be reconceptualized.

In terms of initial impact and lasting significance within and beyond the discipline, the emergence of Marxist and other radical philosophies of geography can hardly be overestimated. In contrast with mainstream conceptions of what the "politics" of political geography stood for, Marxist geographers (such as David Harvey, Doreen Massey, Richard Peet, Neil Smith, and many others) began to situate explanations of territory (and space and place more generally) within the historical processes of capital accumulation, industrial production, labor relations, uneven development, and consumption (Storper and Scott 1986; Storper and Walker 1989). Territories have increasingly come to be seen as reflecting, reinforcing, or undermining the workings of more pervasive social forces and not simply as the containers of sovereign authority. "Territorialization," writes Harvey, "is, in the end, an outcome of political struggles and decisions made in the context of technological and political-economic conditions" (2000, 75). Marxist geographers also link normative assessments of these processes to explicit concerns for social justice and the experiential human suffering entailed by capitalist modes of production and social regulation. Territorial configurations in a capitalist political economy, then, are not confined to two-dimensional, static containers. They may not even be mappable by conventional cartographic methods. Rather, they are constituted by shifting mosaics that reflect, reinforce, reproduce, and, at times, undermine the processes intrinsic to capital accumulation. In an influential piece entitled "The Geopolitics of Capitalism" (1985) Harvey writes that "the inner contradictions of capitalism are expressed through the restless formation and reformation of geographical landscapes. This is the tune to which the historical geography of capitalism [and its associated territorializations and re-territorializations] must dance without cease" (p. 150). This process applies to and is legible in large scale social-spatial processes such as state formation (and deformation), colonialism, and decolonization, as well as smaller-scale, locally expressed processes of investment and disinvestment, and the micro-territorializing processes associated with segmenting labor markets and regimenting or deregimenting work places.

A particularly useful idea that has been employed by many critical geographers and which has significant implications for understanding the workings of territoriality is that of "the production of space." This notion was formulated initially by the French Marxist philosopher Henri Lefebvre. It begins with the premise that social space – including, but not limited to territorial configurations – "is a (social) product ... space thus produced also serves as a tool of thought and action ... it is also a means of control, and hence of domination and power; yet...it escapes in part those who would make use of it" (1991, 26). Many scholars have found Lefebvre's distinction between "representations of space" and "spatial representations" particularly useful. *Representations of space* refer to "conceptualized space, the space of scientists, planners, urbanists, technocrats and social engineers" (p. 38), while *representational spaces* signify "space as directly lived through its associated images and symbols, and hence, the space of inhabitants" (p. 39). This distinction might capture that between how territory is imagined and represented by practitioners of conventional IR, geopolitics, statecraft, collectivization or decollectivization, planning, and by real-estate lawyers and judges, on the one hand, and how it is experienced by migrants, refugees, occupying soldiers, or tenants on the other. It could be argued that many of the perspectives on territory that we surveyed in the first part of this chapter exemplify Lefebvrian *representations of space*. The workings of territory may be partly understood with reference to the tensions or contradictions between these divergent (and antagonistic) dispositions toward space and the practices that these contradictions condition. With specific reference to the territorializations of the sovereign state and the regime of liberal property ownership, Lefebvre would direct our attention to the contradiction "between the appearance of security and the constant threat, and indeed, occasional irruption of violence" (p. 53).

The Production of Space provides innumerable resources for the reconceptualization of territoriality. For the purposes of this Short Introduction I will focus only on the collapse of the ontological distinction between territory (or "space" more generally) and "society," and the emergence of more *constitutive* notions such as "spatialities" or "the socio-spatial" that inform much of contemporary critical geography. Edward Soja, for example, drawing on and interpreting Lefebvre, has contributed to the deconstruction of the inherited distinction between "society" and "space." He writes that "to be alive is to participate in the social production of space, to shape and be shaped by a constantly evolving spatiality which concretizes social action and relationship" (1985, 90). "[S]ocial life", he asserts, "is both space forming and space contingent" (p. 94). Soja developed and extended some of these ideas in his highly influential *Postmodern Geographies* (1989). The point for us is that, in the 1970s and 1980s, territory began to be understood not as a passive grid of lines and spaces that simply differentiate various containers of the social, but rather as inextricably implicated one way or another in virtually all aspects of human social action, being, consciousness and experience.

Another significant development in social thought that has necessitated a rethinking of the mutual constitutivity of "the spatial" and "the social" is the development and proliferation of feminist modes of socio-spatial analysis and critique. Feminist geographers, and feminists in other fields with an interest in the relationship between space, power, and experience, tend not to thematize relations in terms of territory as such, preferring to write instead about space and place. I suggest, though, that feminist understandings of space and power are indispensable for a clearer view of how territory has been reconceptualized – and for a clearer view of how territory is practiced and experienced (Aiken et al. 1998; McDowell and Sharp 1997).

Domosh and Seager's *Putting Women in Place* (2001), for example, traces the relationships between gender, sexuality, patriarchy, and the historical spatialization of social life at various scales of experience and imagination. Many of the most significant aspects of their analysis center on what others would call territorializations: the gendered separation of "work" and "home," the dichotomized spatialization of "public" and "private," and the gendered division of labor. They also examine the territorialization of urban space, with its characteristic exclusions and restrictions, and the constitutive role of gender ideologies (and differential experiences) in the projects of nationalism, colonialism, and imperialism. These all demonstrate the dense and shifting territorial configurations within which lives – women's and men's – are lived.

Feminist analyses of the gendered history and politics of social space extend our understandings of the complex relationships of power, ideology, experience and various forms of territorialization. A significant contribution is the greater awareness that questions of gender and sexuality have been systematically excluded from nearly all conventional – as well as from very many "critical" – examinations of territory. Feminist readings of territoriality also explore how historical and culturally variable forms of gendered territorialities intersect with and condition other social forces, even as they require us to revise inherited conceptions of "work," "the political," or "the subject." Finally, they provide resources for conceptualizing expressions and practices of territory at all scales of analysis from the intra-corporeal (vaginal, uteral) to the global. Feminist spatial studies have also opened up ways of rethinking these connections in other power contexts, such as those centered on sexual orientation, race, disability, and age.

Culture theory

Another interdisciplinary project that has had a considerable influence on the recent reconceptualization of territory is culture theory, and, more specifically, border theory. Culture theory, as I am using the term, emerged out of developments in anthropology in which anthropologists began to critically examine conventional conceptions of culture in ways that are analogous to the reassessment of "sovereignty" in IR, "space" in geography, and "politics" in feminism. As with other interdisciplinary projects, this has led to a re-evaluation of how taken-for-granted representations of territory have conditioned received views of core themes of these disciplines. Reciprocally, newer understandings of space and culture have also influenced critical IR theory and critical geography, especially in debates about the significance of globalization.

Gupta and Ferguson, in "Beyond 'Culture': Space, Identity and the Politics of Difference" (1997a), criticize the "assumed isomorphism of space, place and culture" (p. 34) and direct attention instead to "a world where identities are increasingly coming to be, if not wholly deterritorialized, at least differently territorialized" (p. 37). This is a world where " 'here' and 'there' become blurred" (p. 38). These authors attempt to reveal what conventional territorial representations of culture and identity obscure. That is to say, they critique a cultural version of the territorial trap. First, inherited discourses of culture and identity tend to ignore "those who inhabit the border, that 'narrow strip along steep edges' of national boundaries . . . The fiction of cultures as discrete, object-like phenomena occupying discrete spaces becomes implausible for those who inhabit the borderlands" (p. 34). Second, disciplinary discourses assume a large measure of cultural homogeneity and obscure or ignore aspects of heterogeneity *within* territorial spaces. For example, "The idea of 'subcultures' attempts to preserve the idea of distinct 'cultures' while acknowledging the relation of different cultures to a dominant culture within the same geographical and territorial space" (p. 35). In this way cultural heterogeneity is contained and domesticated by state-centered conceptions of territory. Third, these ways of imagining territory make investigations of the cultural dynamics of post-coloniality difficult. Gupta and Ferguson ask, "To which places do the hybrid cultures of post-coloniality belong? Does the colonial encounter create a 'new culture' in both the colonized and colonizing country, or does it destabilize the notion that nations and cultures are isomorphic? . . . [P]ost-coloniality problematizes the relationship between space and culture" (p. 35). Post-colonial theory thereby makes conventional understandings of the relationship less useful for making sense of either culture or political territory. Repudiating the assumption of isomorphism between territory and culture opens up a host of new questions and problems that have been obscured by the unexamined work that territory accomplishes in conventional discourses. "The special challenge," they assert, " . . . is to use a focus on the way space is imagined (but not imaginary) as a way to explore the mechanisms through which such conceptual processes of place making [and territorializations] meet the changing global economic and political conditions of lived spaces." They suggest that,

> Instead of stopping with the notion of de-territorialization, the pulveriza-
> tion of the space of high modernity, we need to theorize how space is being
> *re*-territorialized in the contemporary world ... Physical location and phys-
> ical territory, for so long the *only* grid on which cultural differences could be
> mapped, need to be replaced by the multiple grids that enable us to see that
> connections and contiguity ... vary considerably by factors such as class,
> gender, race, and sexuality and are differently available to those in different
> locations in the field of power. (1997a, 50)

One highly influential attempt to provide such a "multiple grid" is to be found in Arjun Appadurai's work on cultural globalization. "Deterri-torialization," he writes, " ... is one of the central features of the modern world" (1990, 11). Privileging mobility over static spaces, he sketches various "dimensions of cultural flows" concerning differences among how people, things, money, images, and ideas circulate throughout the globe, through the territorial grid of nation-states, intersecting with each other to create complex "landscapes" or "imagined worlds." These "dis-junctive" landscapes – and the "cultural politics of deterritorialization" (p. 13) that they occasion – are often radically discrepant with the con-ventional, state-centered territorializations of power and identity. Taking all of this into account requires that "we begin to think of the configur-ation of cultural forces in today's world as fundamentally fractal, that is, as possessing no Euclidean boundaries, structures or regularities" (p. 20). "[W]e need to combine a fractal metaphor for the shape of cultures (in the plural) with a polythetic account of their overlaps and resemblances" (p. 20).

Border theory

> Territorial borders both shape and are shaped by what they contain, and
> what crosses or is prevented from crossing them. The "container" and the
> "contents" are mutually formative. Ultimately, the significance of borders
> derives from the importance of territoriality as an organizing principle
> of political and social life. The functions and meanings of borders have
> always been inherently ambiguous and contradictory; and these character-
> istics seem to take on a new salience with claims about emerging "border-
> less worlds" and the "space of places" giving way to the "space of flows."
> (Anderson and O'Dowd 1999, 594)

Formally, as Anderson and O'Dowd argue, the meaning and practical significance of territory is a function of the meaning and pragmatics of borders. "Territoriality," they continue, "necessarily produces and focuses attention on borders. It is embodied in the modern, sovereign, 'territorial nation-state' " (1999, 598). One of the more significant contemporary interdisciplinary projects concerning territory is border theory, which can be understood, in part, as a convergence of the newer IR theory and culture theory. A strong presence in anthropology, it also draws on and informs many other projects and seeks to understand connections among culture, politics, economics, and experience in social space. Border theory, like other projects we have surveyed, repudiates the conventional vision of borders as marking the sharp edges of homogenous territories and the ways in which these conventional views locate what is beyond borders as "outside" and dangerous. It is premised on the rejection of the ways in which borderlines are understood as demarcating self-evident otherness. Instead, in border theory, the margins are centered and the focus is on borderlands as sites of mixing or hybridity.

> [C]loser critical scrutiny of borders challenges their reification and reveals them as far from simple. Instead, they appear inherently contradictory, problematical, and multifaceted. They are at once gateways and barriers to the "outside world," protective and imprisoning, areas of opportunity and/or insecurity, zones of contact and/or conflict, of co-operation and/or competition, of ambivalent identities and/or aggressive assertion of difference. These apparent dichotomies may alternate with time and place, but – more interestingly – they can co-exist simultaneously in the same people, some of whom have to regularly deal not with one state but two. (Anderson and O'Dowd 1999, 595–596)

As with some of the other interdisciplinary projects, border theory departs from a static, cartographic vision of territory and emphasizes a variety of cross-border flows and mobilities such as those associated with migrant workers (seasonal, daily, in the life-cycle), refugees, tourists, and smugglers. If borders are understood as the most active sites of territorial complexes, then our attention is directed to a wider range of territorial practices and to dimensions of the workings of power other than those conventional theory provides. These may include formal state practices such as those involving "border control," checkpoints, customs windows, surveillance, exclusion, inclusion, expulsion, and regulation. They also include practices of evasion, negotiation, and resistance of various forms. Many scholars have explored the relationship between borderlands and cultural hybridity, or the question of multiple or fluid identities in relation to borders (Flynn 1997; French 2002; Rösler and Wendl 1999; Wilson and Donnan 1998). Gupta and Ferguson, for example, reject understanding a border in terms of "a fixed topographical site between two other fixed locales (nations, societies, cultures)," and instead view the border as "an interstitial zone of displacement and deterritorialization that shapes the identity of the hybridized subject." Indeed, they say, the border is "the normal 'locale' of the postmodern subject" (1997a, 18).

These ideas have obvious implications for any understanding of territory – at least with respect to the territoriality of nation-states. Even granting the continued efficacy of many state territorial practices – as evinced, for example, by the militarization of that most scrutinized borderland involving Mexico and the US (Alvarez 1999; Kearny 1998; Ortiz 2001; Palafox 2000) (and by the fact that, claims of de-territorialization notwithstanding, many of the mobile, "hybrid" participants themselves may hold more conventional views about the isomorphism of culture, politics, and territory) – post-modern border theory emphasizes the disjunctures, overlaps, and instabilities among territories organized around often incompatible ideas and practices. It is precisely these features that are commonly obscured or denied by conventional disciplinary discourses and the unreflective privileging of statist conceptions of territory.

But if borderlands, instead of marking fixity, certainty, stability, and mutual exclusivity are seen as generating fluidity, ambiguity, and mutual constitutivity, where, one might ask, is the border of the borderlands? One answer is "nowhere." In "Race, Space and the Reinvention of Latin America in Mexican Chicago" (1998), Nicholas De Genova finds all of the features of the border in the heartland. "[I]t is increasingly difficult to imagine that Latin America [and Mexico and the "Third World"] begins only at the border and increasingly necessary to discern the racialized boundaries of the space of the U.S. nation state imploded deep within its territorial map." The border, he finds, "is everywhere" inside the United States (1998, 106). It is also, therefore, "everywhere" within the territorial space of Mexico. But this is not a thesis about the *disappearance* of boundaries, it is a mapping of their *proliferation and dispersal* throughout social, political, and economic spaces. It is, ultimately, a thesis about social space itself. And if the US–Mexico border is to be found at various sites throughout the spaces of the US and Mexico then one might be able to consider the sites of the US–Guatemalan border, the Pakistani–Canadian border, or the US–Afghani border. One might also consider territorial phenomena such as the Indian–Pakistani border as it may be differentially encountered in London, Kuwait City, or Los Angeles. And here, perhaps, we have encountered the complete inversion – or perversion – of conventional understandings of territory.

But it is not quite complete. Another important theme of border studies that breaks with conventional views is the emphasis on the effects of borders and territory on "everyday life" and on embodied experiences. This begins to bring into focus the complex boundaries between "the state" and "the subject" or, as Wilson and Donnan put it, "how people experience the nation and the state in their everyday lives at international borders" (1999, xiii). The turn toward "everyday life" is expressed in connection with IR theory by Michael Niemann, who argues, "lived experiences, rather than being the residue left over after the machinations of 'grand politics' have played themselves out, are a crucial component of international relations and . . . our theoretical understanding of the field will remain incomplete unless the experiences of everyday life are incorporated" (2003, 115). Or, as Roxeanne Doty puts it in "Desert Tracts: Statecraft in Remote Places," "There are human beings who may have never heard the word statecraft, and yet their lives are deeply implicated in this non-thing, this process, this practice, this desire that so deeply occupies the consciousness of statesmen and IR scholars" (2001, 526). "These people and their dreams," she continues, "disturb the project of statecraft, a project that requires unambiguous boundaries that evoke a secure sense of knowing just who 'we' are" (p. 527). "These people know about deserts and thirst and suffocating heat. They know that borders mean everything and nothing. Life is pounding against the world's borders, straining their edges" (p. 538). Here it might be recalled that more Mexicans die crossing the border every year than American soldiers were killed in Iraq before "victory" was declared in May 2003. "As for territory," writes Achille Mbembe, "it is fundamentally an intersection of moving bodies. It is defined essentially by the set of movements that take place within it. Seen this way, it is a set of possibilities that historically situated actors constantly resist or realize" (2000, 261).

It is with respect to bodies and embodied subjectivity – to feeling the effects of thirst and heat, to being chased, captured, rounded up, and delivered – that perhaps we can see both the ultimate collapse of conventional notions of territory *and* the continued efficacy of the state practices premised on these notions. Wilson and Donnan write of "those forces that demarcate geographical and political space as lines on the map simultaneously inscribe the body's topography" (1999, 129). Policing the flow of goods and people "may also involve searches of a more personal and intimate kind . . . at the most extreme, such searches of the person may involve a 'strip search.' This requires the removal of clothing for detailed examination and even a probing of the body itself" (p. 130).

Such practices reinforce the idea that the border checkpoints and custom posts are liminal spaces, ones within which the usual western conventions of bodily contact cease to apply...They are liminal spaces within which state power is absolute, and can be imposed upon even that most intimate element of our being, our body...In the final analysis, even our bodies are no longer ours in such settings, their agency displaced by the raw power of the state which can be revealed there. (p. 131)

They continue, "the boundaries of the body become analogous to the borders of the nation and the nation-state; both are vulnerable to penetration and corruption from the outside, susceptible to disease and alien intrusion respectively" (p. 136). Here we see how the macro-territories of IR theory and the "territories of the self," particularly Goffman's "sheath," may interpenetrate each other, even if they are not versions of each other.

Globalization

In many ways border theory, culture theory, critical geography and post-structuralist international relations theory are all responses to (or aspects of) broader interdisciplinary engagements with globalization. Globalization here is understood both as a set of processes and as a set of discourses about changing conditions in the world. As with other themes under discussion in this chapter, it is a deeply contested concept (Brawley 2003; Schimato and Webb 2003). At the most basic and least contentious level of description globalization refers to "the expanding scale, growing magnitude, speeding up and deepening impact of transcontinental flows and patterns of social interaction. It refers to a shift or transformation in the scale of human organization that links distant communities and expands the reach of power relations across the world's regions and continents" (Held and McGrew 2002). The focus of attention is on those processes through which various social, economic, political, and cultural phenomena that had, until recently, been operative on more or less local, national, or regional scales have become (more or less) ubiquitous on a planetary scale. These include everything from industrial production to cultural identity; legal consciousness to cuisine; financial transactions to social movements; chatrooms to paramilitary corporations. Looked at this way, globalization is taken to entail delocalization, or the uncoupling of social phenomena and locale or "place." While the causes, effects, and historicity of globalization are debated, it is commonly noted that its intensification in the late twentieth century was facilitated by dramatic changes in the technologies of transportation and communication, especially air travel and the internet. But for our purposes it is more significant that globalization is also commonly taken to entail de-territorialization. That is, social phenomena that had been understood as having been contained or constrained by (usually national) territorial structures are now no longer as easily cabined by these structures. From this perspective globalization is bringing into being an increasingly "borderless world" (Ohmae 1999). As we have already seen, this is a world characterized by the prominence of flows and networks that are relatively unimpeded by territoriality. To the extent that territory and sovereignty are correlated, globalization also seems to entail the obsolescence of the state (Cusimano 2000; Hudson 1999). Jan Aart Scholte, for example, writes,

> Globalization calls into question the prevailing territorialist ontology of modern social theory. This entrenched supposition holds that social space is plotted in terms of locations, distances and borders in a three-dimensional geography. Yet globality introduces a new quality of social space, one that is effectively non-territorial and distance-less . . . Globalization has made the identification of boundaries . . . more problematic than ever. To this extent, a new, non-territorialist cartography of social life is needed. (1996, 48–49)

Neil Brenner agrees that globalization has rendered "the container-like qualities of states . . . highly problematic" (1999, 40), yet in a brilliant investigation of territoriality under these conditions he rejects the reading of de-territorialization that this commonly implies. Crucial to his analysis is a sophisticated appreciation of the significance of the verticality or scale of territoriality in the contemporary world. "Globalization," he says, "unfolds simultaneously upon multiple, intertwined geographical scales – not only within global space, but through the production, differentiation, reconfiguration, and transformation of sub-global spaces such as territorial states, regions, cities and localities" (p. 44). Given our earlier discussion of bodies and borders we might note that these are not the only spaces through which the processes associated with globalization unfold. Brenner sees interpretations such as Scholte's as expressing a sort of "global territorialism" that "represent[s] global space in a state-centric manner, as a pre-given territorial container within which globalization unfolds" (p. 59) and as, in essence, the "territorial state writ large" (p. 61). Central to Brenner's analysis is the argument that de-territorializations on one scale or at one time entail *re-territorializations* on other scales or at other times (p. 43).

> Today state territoriality is increasingly intertwined with and superimposed upon various emergent spatial forms . . . that cannot be described adequately as contiguous, mutually exclusive, and self-enclosed blocks of

space ... [S]tate institutions are ... being radically re-scaled at once upward, downward, and outward to create polymorphic layers of state territorial organization ... Under these circumstances, the image of global social space as a complex mosaic of superimposed and interpenetrating nodes, levels, scales, and morphologies has become more appropriate than the traditional Cartesian model of homogenous, interlinked blocks of territory associated with the modern interstate system. (Brenner 1999, 69)

For Brenner, then, "globalization" names a real and complex phenomenon that does have profound effects on contemporary and emerging forms of territoriality. But it does not entail the appearance of a "borderless" or de-territorialized world. Far from it. As with De Genova's reading of the US–Mexico border, globalization signifies the proliferation of heterogenous borders and territories and their fluid articulation across a range of scales. Accepting these newer conceptions of territoriality, however, does render analysis much more difficult. In an important sense territoriality has escaped the confines of (state-centric) territorialism without obliterating those inherited structures. Territoriality in the twenty-first century is a potentially limitless system of limits.

Concluding Remarks

This rough guide to the ways in which the scholarly examination of territory has changed reveals that a topic that once seemed relatively simple and obvious has become rather complicated and contested. The heightened sense of complexity is, in part, the product of increasingly interdisciplinary approaches to the topic. It is no doubt also a reflection of changes in the territorialization of the worlds that scholars and commentators (and everyone else) inhabit and try to make sense of. Massive socio-spatial transformations associated with, for example, processes of colonialism, imperialism, world wars, local wars, and cold wars, decolonization, urbanization, liberation struggles, globalization, and the unending revolutions in communication and transportation pretty much guarantee continuous territorial reconfigurations at all scales of experience and analysis. These seem to require continual reflection and rethinking.

3

Human Territoriality and its Boundaries

Introduction

In the last chapter I surveyed a range of approaches to territoriality from some key disciplines and noted the recent tendency to release the topic from the constraints of these disciplinary perspectives. Absent from that account was any discussion of the singularly most significant book-length treatment of the topic, Robert Sack's *Human Territoriality: Its Theory and History* (1986). It is fair to say that *Human Territoriality* is unprecedented in its scope, focus, and analytic ambition. In many ways it remains unsurpassed. Indeed, less than 15 years after its publication it was recognized as a "classic text" in human geography and a seminal inspiration for subsequent researchers (Agnew 2000; Paasi 2000b). Unlike most work on territory that preceded it, Sack's approach was vigorously interdisciplinary, drawing on anthropology, economics, history, political theory, sociology, and his home discipline of human geography. It may be of interest that, although Sack situated his work within the sub-fields of social geography and historical geography he did not do so with respect to political geography, the sub-field that, until then, was most centrally concerned with issues of territory. Perhaps this was intended as a gesture of liberation, but it may also be indicative, as I will discuss more fully below, of a relative absence of concern with the political in *Human Territoriality*.

Among the principal strengths of *Human Territoriality* is its fluid applicability to all scales of social reality from the interpersonal to the international. Another feature that, for some, may be a strength but, for others, a weakness, is its explicit neutrality with respect to social theories. The book is also notable for its deep historicity. Indeed, as signaled by the subtitle, *Human Territoriality* is nearly as concerned with illuminating the flow (or rupture) of time as with the organization of social space. *Human*

Territoriality presents a number of historical narratives which explore the continuities and transformations of territorial structures. A key theme that organizes the book is modernity and its distinctiveness vis-à-vis the pre-modern. With respect to this theme, reading *Human Territoriality* through 20 years of subsequent work on the topic one is struck by how much has changed. From around the time that *Human Territoriality* was published through the 1990s modernity itself was subjected to a very different sort of analysis. Scholars from virtually all of the social sciences and humanities began to imagine modernity in distinctively *un*modern ways: as having an end, if not having ended. Reading *Human Territoriality* through the prism (or fog, depending on one's point of view) of concerns with post-modernity reveals a number of assumptions and commitments about the world and about knowledge that inform the book.

In the following pages I will first present a chapter-by-chapter overview of the book. Any book (including the present one) is necessarily a product of its time, place, and the commitments of its author. In the second half of the chapter I will examine these contextual aspects not so much as limits or limitations but merely to indicate some of the boundaries of *Human Territoriality* as revealed by subsequent formulations of territory, such as those discussed in the previous chapter. If *Human Territoriality* was, in the mid-1980s, an unparalleled achievement for helping us to see, see around, and see through territory, more recent engagements enable us to see this perspective itself in a different light. They allow us to ask what is foregrounded and backgrounded, centered and marginalized in Sack's account. It should go without saying that examining any work from within a different set of assumptions does not in itself constitute negative criticism unless one shares these alternative commitments. Indeed, features that, from one perspective, may be regarded as vices may, from another point of view, be the very virtues that make a work of continued relevance and utility. I will be limiting my remarks solely to the text of *Human Territoriality* and will not trace developments in Sack's subsequent and substantial contributions to geographical, social, and ethical theory (Sack 1997, 2003). I will then examine the book in terms of four themes that have emerged as more or less central to more recent debates about territoriality: the nature(s) of modernity; discourse and representation; identity; and politics. Politics, of course, is not in itself a new preoccupation in social thought. However, politics is now understood somewhat differently in light of questions about modernity, discourse, and identity and these, in turn, reflect on how territory may be understood. Moreover, if there is one general criticism of *Human Territoriality* it is that, while the concept of power is a central – indeed, definitional – theme, politics in any robust sense is virtually absent.

Overview

In his introduction Sack takes us into the territory of territoriality: "Previous scholarship," he writes, had until then "only skirted its perimeters" (p. 1). This being an initial foray, he makes no claim that *Human Territoriality* can be more than "a sketch" and an invitation for further exploration. While the book far exceeds the modest aim of ground clearing and surveying, this self-limitation is important to keep in mind when we later examine themes and issues that are not covered. Significantly, his opening move is to sharply distinguish *human* territoriality from territorial behavior as it may be observed in non-human animals (or plants, for that matter). As we saw in chapter 2, some authors make precisely the opposite assumption. Among the features that make human territoriality unique for Sack are some of the attributes commonly thought to make us distinctively human: intentionality, complex communication, open-ended historicity, the creation of institutions, and the like. For us territoriality is not "biologically motivated, but rather . . . socially and geographically rooted" (p. 2). This is not simply a claim about origins but, crucially, a claim about explanation. Unlike theories that assimilate human territoriality to instinct or biological imperatives, seeing *through* territory, for Sack, entails examining it in specifically social, historical, or cultural frames of reference. That is, Sack's task is to denaturalize territory.

Meanings

Chapter 1, "The Meaning of Territory," begins to more fully stake out the terrain of Sack's theory and history by way of definitional contrasts. He sets off with an initial approximate definition. "Territoriality for humans is a powerful strategy to control people and things by controlling area" (p. 5). It is, necessarily, a relational concept. It is about people controlling people. It is inextricably bound to power (control). It is strategic. One primary aim of the book, then, is to "analy[ze] the possible advantages and disadvantages that territoriality can provide" (p. 5). Stated this way it seems to be immaterial as to whether these advantages and disadvantages accrue to the people who are controlling or the people who are the objects of control. Sack also introduces the key themes of history and modernity. Through a set of diachronic studies he demonstrates "that some territorial effects are universal, occurring in practically any historical context and social organization, that others are specific to particular historical periods and organizations, and that only modern society tends to use the entire range of possible effects" (p. 6). One of the advantages of exploring territoriality in connection with modernity is that it can "help us unravel the meanings and implications of modernity and the future role of territoriality" (p. 6). By way of demonstrating the centrality of the theme of modernity the bulk of chapter 1 consists of three detailed illustrations. The first, and most elaborate, examines the changes in the use of territory among (or in relation to) the Chippewa peoples of central North America from the pre-contact (pre-modern) era through the period of contact with and conquest by Euro-Americans. The second and third illustrations treat instances of micro-territoriality in modern life – the home and the workplace.

The principal elements of Chippewa uses of territoriality, in Sack's example, derive from elements of social structure and the economics of resource use. He describes the Chippewa as having no organized political structure resembling a modern state. Their social organization is centered around autonomous "bands." They are largely engaged in hunting and gathering activities (and, in the southern part of their area, some subsistence agriculture) and are socially egalitarian. Egalitarianism here refers to the absence of economic stratification based on class. Other axes of inequality, such as those of age, gender, or clan, are not considered. In the pre-contact period the Chippewa were "minimally territorial" (p. 7) in Sack's sense of the term.

The area occupied by Chippewa peoples fluctuated seasonally and over years. It was not a clearly bounded territory vis-à-vis other Native peoples. Neither was there extensive territorialization inside their communities. Even garden plots "were not clearly demarcated and fenced-in territories" (p. 8). It should be noted that, given the complexity of any social order, there may indeed have been aspects of territoriality that escaped Sack's attention. Nonetheless, this vision of the social organization of space helps one to imagine the processes by which more – or different – expressions of territoriality might come into being. In a thought experiment Sack introduces changes arising both outside and inside of the social structure of Chippewa life, such as scarcity of resources for hunters or greater emphasis on agriculture, that might create conditions under which some people might find it "convenient" (p. 8) to fence in fields, for example, or otherwise use territoriality more intensively. Or an imagined increase in population that results in crowding might lead to more rigid rules regarding the allocation of garden plots. Pushing a bit further, Sack asks the reader to imagine that, under such conditions, "a ruling family [could] emerge claiming access to some or all of the community's resources" (p. 9). Under these conditions of increasing hierarchy or stratification, "territoriality would be an extremely useful device to affect [the ruling family's] claims" (p. 9). The principal point of this speculative exercise is to reinforce the fundamental idea that social life and social structure are inseparable from territoriality. As it happens, while this model may have applied to other pre-modern peoples, more important for the Chippewa, as for other indigenous peoples of the world, was the arrival of strangers with strange ideas of territory – and of classification, communication, and enforcement.

Social and economic changes whose genesis was in Europe, its colonies on the Atlantic coast, or in Mexico came at first rather indirectly. The arrival of horses, diseases, Native peoples from the East engaged in trapping furs for the European market, and the odd group of explorers brought profound transformations to Chippewa life. These agents were clearly no respecters of the territoriality of Chippewa people. Sack here speculates as to whether these changes induced an increasing sense of proprietorship over hunting grounds. As Native peoples of the East were themselves forced westward by European expropriation and settlement, other changes occurred that had a bearing on territoriality. Of great import were the different ways that the moderns of the East *imagined* territory. As we all know, the land that was to become "America" was imagined to have been "discovered" by Europeans. And though others had no notion that they had been discovered, the moderns of "the Age of Exploration" claimed to possess what they had never seen, or indeed, even had little reason to know existed. Possessory and sovereignty claims were registered by the rulers of European states in relation to each other, not, initially, in relation to indigenous peoples, now collectively identified as "Indians." And from these "claims" devolved "grants" to colonists, and from these grants devolved further sub-grants to speculators and settlers. Again, these territorial assertions were relative to other speculators and settlers. This novel way of territorializing the life-worlds of the Chippewa people (and many others) might have remained more fantastic than real were it not for the ways in which these territorialized conceptions of "sovereignty" and "property" were imposed on indigenous peoples. Sack writes that, "with the stroke of a pen, Americans of European descent were to classify, divide and control people, including the Chippewa, based solely on their location in space" (p. 11). But, we might note, it was not the pen so much as the musket and the smallpox-infected trade goods that were decisive. With respect to the transformations of territory, Sack emphasizes the processes and practices of surveying, partitioning, sub-dividing, and privatizing land along with the establishment of national, state, and local political territories as most important. Within a comparatively short time the imprint of a very different kind of territoriality was inscribed onto this part of the world.

To heighten the contrast between pre-modern and modern territorial practices Sack takes us to an imagined contemporary home and workplace in Wisconsin, a part of the Chippewa homeland. While the people we meet here are not racially identified, there is no reason to assume that some of them, at least, are not themselves Chippewa. In the first example a stay-at-home dad is doing housework while his two small children are attempting to "help" by doing the dishes – a task that is clearly beyond their capabilities. Recognizing their good intentions as well as their incompetence – and valuing the integrity of the dishware – he sees that he has two choices. He can explain to them why they shouldn't be doing that or he can simply declare the kitchen "off limits." The second exemplifies territoriality as an assertion of control over an area. This example also illustrates the fact that a place "can be a territory at one time and not another" (p. 16). Before the parental injunction the kitchen was simply a room; now, infused with prohibition, it is a territory. (One might, however, imagine other more extreme territorial strategies such as locking the children in a closet or banishing them to the street.) Though part of the purpose of this illustration is to contrast the pre-modern and the distinctively modern, one can well imagine pre-contact Chippewa parents telling their children to keep out of some well-defined space.

The final example in chapter 1 sketches a workplace in which a secretary is required to stay at his designated "work station." He may be free to move occasionally through the hallways or into the coffee room or men's room (and stalls) but he is not free to enter offices. And were he to abuse his privileges of mobility by, say, hanging out in the mail room, he could be subject to the ultimate territorial sanction – being expelled from the workplace by termination. "For the secretary, territoriality acts as a physical restraint" (p. 17). After five o'clock the building is, indeed, off-limits to most of the employees. The custodian, however, may have access to every room in the building. But here, one imagines, the micro-territories of desk drawers and envelopes remain beyond the threshold of exploration. This is, in many ways, a prototypic modern territorial con-figuration in which access is determined by reference to a combination of roles and rules, conceptions of ownership and authority, and culturally specific conceptions of metrical time.

Chapter 1 concludes with a fuller definition of territoriality: "the at-tempt by an individual or group to affect, influence, or control people, phenomena, and relationships, by delimiting and asserting control over a geographical area" (p. 19). Here Sack also distinguishes territory from the related concepts of "place" and "region" and notes other nuances of his conception. For example, he notes that territories can change and they can occur in degrees. "A maximum security prison is more territorial than a cell in a county jail, which is more territorial than a room in a half way house" (p. 20). The intensity of territory seems to be a function of the intensity of control or power.

Theory

Chapter 2, "Theory," is the most original and useful part of the book. More an analytical framework than a theory as such, it serves as a sort of field guide or "How to" for seeing the effects or consequences of territorial operations. Again, the framework is constructed in such a way as to not be constrained by specific types of territories such as nation-states, rooms, or voting districts. The sense of "theory" also pertains to Sack's explicit neutrality with respect to other, then prominent, social theories, particularly Weberian understandings of modern organizations and neo-Marxism. Sack offers his theory as one that is "empirical and logical" (p. 28), and draws heuristic analogies with theorization in the physical sciences. But because the effects of territoriality "pertain to people, not to atoms, they are more appropriately termed potential 'reasons' or causes of, or potential 'consequences or effects' of territoriality" (p. 28). This is important not only for the task of denaturalizing human territoriality, but, as I will discuss later, for justifying assumptions that are made about human beings, particularly our instrumental, rational disposition toward the world and each other. Also important is his recognition that, while this or that particular occurrence of territorial behavior may implicate normativity or moral issues, territoriality *per se* is normatively neutral. It can be used for malicious, benign, or ethically indifferent purposes (reasons). The theory, then, must also strive to maintain moral, political, and ideological indifference. "[T]he theory itself will not present procedures by which one can judge whether an action is, on its own merits, good or bad" (p. 31). This, of course, does not prevent one from applying Sack's framework in order to explicate or advance normative claims.

The "atomic structure" (p. 29) of territoriality consists of 10 "tendencies" and 14 "primary combinations" of tendencies understood as potential effects of the strategy. Any instance of territoriality can be analyzed with respect to the presence, absence, or relative importance of these ingredients. The first three tendencies have already been introduced. They are part of the definition: classification by area, communication, and enforcement. The tendencies are given numbers for clarity of presentation. The definitional tendencies (1, 2, 3) are always present. The seven "potential" tendencies (4–10) are more contingent.

1   In elaborating on **classification by area** Sack emphasizes the advantages of declaring an area off-limits compared to enumerating each of the things inside of the territory to which access is prohibited. Thus, territoriality can be a generalizing strategy and, as such, may be more convenient or efficient to use. Of course, as we will see,

classification by area pertains to much more than establishing "no go" zones or prohibiting access to things in space.

2   A second principal tendency or "reason" for acting territorially is that, through the use of boundaries, **communication** is made easier.

3   "Territoriality can be the most efficient strategy for **enforcing** control" (p. 32). Again, the emphasis is on the advantages of territorial over non-territorial strategies for effecting access to things or resources. Interestingly, given Sack's explicit anti-naturalizing impulses, the examples used to clarify this tendency refer to animal behavior and not human forms of authority or power.

4   "Territory provides a means of **reifying** power" (p. 32). Because social power is not always visible or tangible, territoriality may have the effect of making it appear so. Territory, through its material signifiers such as fences, gates, border guards, and so on, gives some forms of power a material referent in the world.

5   "Territory can be used to **displace** attention from the relationship between the controller and controlled" (p. 33). Like the tendency toward reification, this may have the effect of obscuring social aspects of power.

6   Relatedly, "Territory helps make relationships **impersonal**" (p. 33) through the technique of having rules apply to spaces (and social roles). Under some conditions territory can have the effect of obscuring personal relationships. Sack uses the example of a prison guard who is responsible for the prisoners in a particular cell block whoever they may be, not for each prisoner as an individual wherever they may be. Similarly, membership (and rights) in a political community are commonly determined by domicile within a territory.

7   Sack identifies a "**place-clearing function**" for territory. This is a rather subtle (or obscure) claim. What seems to be suggested is that under some conditions territory can appear to be a "general, *neutral*, essential means by which a place is made" (p. 33). His example is property rights in land.

8   "Territoriality [or, perhaps more accurately, territory] acts as a **container or mold** for spatial properties of events" (p. 33). This container function (or even its *apparent* function) is extremely important for limiting the scope of such phenomena as political authority, sovereignty, rights, and responsibilities and for underwriting spatial definitions of identity.

9   Under certain conditions, especially those associated with modernity, territoriality "helps to create the idea of **socially emptiable space**" (p. 33). That is, conceiving of segments of social space as territories or spatial containers facilitates the further conceptualization of these as "full" or "empty." So a vacant lot or a "no man's

land," while not literally devoid of material contents, can be viewed
as such, and this conceptualization can, in turn, inform behavior.
10 Territories are prolific. **"Territory can help engender more territoriality"** (p. 34). This proliferation effect, accomplished through, say,
subdivision or combination, is particularly important with respect to
the territorial constitution of hierarchies.

These 10 "tendencies," presented in list form here as in *Human Territoriality*, represent key findings. Some are rather obvious, indeed, definitional; some express more novel insights into the workings of
territoriality. Each is rather abstract and subtle. This abstractness is
a virtue and key to the utility of the theory. Each is conceived of as a
basic resource with which to analyze the possible consequences of territoriality in whichever social context we encounter it. The next step in the
theory is to examine a small set of (equally abstract) combinations of these
tendencies in order to see more clearly the finer details of territoriality.

Primary combinations

By elucidating what he sees as "primary combinations" Sack draws our
attention to some of the more significant "logical interrelations among
the tendencies" (p. 34) and their practical effects or uses. As important as
intentionality is for territory as a strategy, it is significant that some of
these primary combination effects (or any of them in a given situation)
may be unintended from the point of view of the controller. Like the
10 tendencies, the 14 primary combinations are presented in list form and
are identified by a lower-case letter (a–n).

a All of the tendencies can enter into the constitution of **complex hierarchies**. For example, classification (1), communication (2), enforcement (3), impersonal relations (6), and molding (8) "can allow for
hierarchical circumscription of knowledge and responsibility, impersonal relationships and strict channels of communication, all of which
are essential components of bureaucracy" (p. 36). Given the ubiquity
of bureaucratic organizations in modern life – from political structures to workplaces, religious organizations, and schools – this indi-
cates that territoriality is vastly more pervasive than most other
scholars had until then assumed.
b The territoriality of complex hierarchical organizations affects the
distribution of knowledge and responsibility within them. It also
facilitates the division of short- and long-term planning functions.
Generally speaking, the higher the "level" of authority within
an organization, the greater the spatial scope of knowledge and

responsibility. Higher levels assume long-range planning functions and lower levels may simply implement these.

c At the "upper echelons of a hierarchy" (p. 36) territories may be used to define subordinate relations through the use of classification (1), enforcement (3), molding (8), and impersonal relations (6). Here Sack makes a distinction between **territorial definitions of social relations** (as in modern political communities) and **social definitions of territorial relations** (as in his pre-modern Chippewa example).

d Given the relationship between hierarchical territoriality and the tendency to promote the circumscription of knowledge, one effect may be an increase in the **efficiency of supervision** of subordinates. Here Sack provides another illustration concerning prisoners and guards: "constraining the movements of prisoners by placing them in their cells makes easier the task of supervising them than if they were allowed to roam freely in the prison" (p. 37).

e Another primary combination related to change is that which gives rise to a sense of **conceptually emptiable space**. "Science, technology, and capitalism make practical the idea of repeatedly and effectively 'filling' and 'emptying' and moving things around within territories of all scales ... territoriality serves as a device to keep space emptiable and fillable" (pp. 37–38). An important element of this capacity to reimagine space is abstractness.

f The possibility of territories taking on what Sack calls **magical** properties follows from a combination of the reifying (4) and displacing (5) tendencies. Perhaps another way of putting this is to say that territories can figure in the mystification of power. In a modern context, "The territory is a physical manifestation of the State's authority, and yet allegiance to territory or homeland makes territory appear as the source of authority" (p. 38).

g **Mismatch** and **spillover** effects may result from circumscribing knowledge and responsibility incorrectly (for the controller's purposes). These appear to be unintended consequences of less than perfectly competent territorializers.

h Somewhat related to magical territoriality (f), displacement (5) and territorial multiplication (10) "make it easier for territory to **appear to be the end rather than the means of control**" (p. 39).

i Territory can "**create inequalities**."

j Various combinations of tendencies enter into the strategy to **divide and control** adversaries or subordinates.

k Another territorial error – or inefficient deployment – concerns the **obscuring of mismatches** between territory and events through the assignment of tasks to the inappropriate level of a territorial hierarchy.

l   "Displacement (5) and territorial multiplication (10) could **direct attention away from the causes of social conflict among territories**" (p. 39). Here Sack offers the example of conflicts between cities and suburbs.

m   Combinations of tendencies can have the effect of **obscuring "the geographical impact of an event"** (p. 39). An example of this may be when people perceive an environmental problem as "local" rather than national or global.

n   Finally, various combinations may be conducive to the process of **secession** or the rise of resistance.

Sack's machinery of "tendencies" and "combinations" is admittedly complicated, and his strategy of purposive abstraction can sometimes hinder understanding. The elements that he emphasizes are concededly not exhaustive and the selection may seem somewhat arbitrary. But these are quibbles. The point, when the theory is viewed as a kind of field guide, is to enable analysts (as well as prospective controllers or those who would resist control) to identify key effects or consequences attending territoriality as a control strategy. Two observations may be in order. First, most of the tendencies and combinations relate to the workings of territoriality in complex hierarchical organizations. This is important insofar as such organizations are pervasive in the modern world and their influence is profound. But, one might argue, there is much more to social life than can be captured by the architecture of bureaucratic organizations. Perhaps too much emphasis on them shifts attention away from other manifestations, uses, or experiences of territory. Second, many of the effects are not directly those of territoriality *per se* so much as the effects of territory *on* perception or consciousness. Displacement, reification, magic, emptiability, and so on are more concerned with how territoriality influences how we see, understand, and misunderstand the world. Of course, the significance of this essential cognitive function of territoriality cannot be underestimated, and it is one of the strengths of *Human Territoriality* to direct our attention to it.

Part II of the theory follows from the recognition that territoriality as a social phenomenon cannot be divorced from a wider understanding of the social order – that is, from sociology or social theory more generally. It also follows from Sack's requirement that his theory be neutral with respect to (and be useful in combination with) the social. In an effort to demonstrate the compatibility of his framework with other understandings of macro-sociological processes, Sack draws out linkages with Weberian sociology and neo-Marxist political economy. It goes without saying that this attempt can be no more than suggestive, and he devotes only a few pages to each. With respect to Weber he discusses territoriality in the context of the internal dynamics of bureaucratic organizations and in connection with the Weberian distinction between "traditional" and "modern" forms of social order. The principal connection to Marxism concerns the obfuscatory combinations of modern territoriality under conditions of class conflict. This part of the theory is less compelling and less relevant than the "atomic structure" outlined in Part I of the theory.

History

The third chapter, "Historical Models: Territoriality, Space and Time", extends the analysis of the fundamental relationship of territoriality and social order through a panoramic survey of 7,000 years of human existence. Sack is aware of the possible drawbacks of this project and is clear about the limited purpose such a survey is intended to serve. In its most general outline, human social organization has taken three forms: the primitive, the modern, and the non-modern civilized. Here Sack neither deprecates primitivity nor celebrates modernity. Likewise, he explicitly dissociates his narrative from any assumptions about progress or necessary "stages" of social development (p. 53). Rather, his specific aim is to identify what he takes to be diagnostic features of these various types of human social organization as they concern the use of territoriality. Nonetheless, when viewed sequentially the central trends that he identifies are: (i) a decrease in the number of autonomous territorial units; (ii) an increase in the size of such units; and (iii) an increase in subdivision or fragmentation of these fewer, larger autonomous units (p. 52). It might be worth asking why "autonomy" emerges here as a central attribute of territory or social order. In the first place, it isn't entirely clear what is meant by autonomy. In the second place, under some conceptions of personhood and its relationship to territory (for example, Goffman's "sheath," discussed in chapter 2 above), it could be argued that, as the number of persons on Earth is orders of magnitude larger now than 7,000 years ago, the number of "autonomous territories" has increased commensurately. These are small points. It does seem that Sack's focus is somewhat narrower here than elsewhere in the book. As with common understandings of modernity, the present era is rather sharply distinguished from the premodern by an increase in the complexity of social order. This complexity is reflected in and furthered by novel uses of territoriality.

Primitive political economy

Drawing largely on secondary sources, Sack constructs an abstract idealtypic model of primitivity. Compared with modernity, the primitive world is much less complex, contains fewer people, and occupies a smaller area. It tends toward an "egalitarian" social structure (again, as in his Chippewa illustration, egalitarianism simply denotes the absence of economic classes). This being the case, reciprocity among familiars plays a prominent role in social relationships. Technology and knowledge are rather more generally accessible than under modernity. Relationships between people and place are imbued with magical or spiritual significance. The occurrence, form, or intensity of territoriality among primitives is strongly conditioned by subsistence economies, where it is used to distribute resources among members of a community. "[T]erritoriality can be expected simply because it can be an efficient device for establishing predictability and density in space and time" (p. 59). That is, one effect of the use of territoriality among primitives is a somewhat greater degree of certainty. Sack also claims that territoriality may be present in such communities under conditions of competition "from outside" (p. 60). But this seems to imply that some notion of territory is already latent so as to allow the identification of "outsiders" and their differentiation from "insiders." Also, for pre-literate peoples territorial boundaries can more effectively "communicate possession and control" (p. 59) than can non-territorial means.

An important aspect of Sack's view of primitive territoriality concerns communal practices of allocation and the rules of land tenure. In his generalized schema "the community," through whatever means or procedures, may allocate plots to members of individual households that constitute the community. The plots that are demarcated may be used but cannot be alienated. Another version of this allocation function occurs when lands are worked communally. He also allows for some mixed systems. "The primitive's use of territoriality supports their basic social organization. When territory occurs at the level of society as a whole, it is used to prevent non-community members from having access to community resources. When it is used within a community, its purpose is to facilitate reciprocity by assigning different but symmetrical tasks to individuals and households" (pp. 62–63).

Perhaps it is unfair to suggest that a selective reading of the anthropological literature cannot sustain such simplifications and the reduction of thousands of "primitive" cultures across the globe and over thousands of years to ideal types. The selection of other accounts, such as the ethnographic accounts mentioned in chapter 2 above, would reveal vastly more varied and complicated ways of being territorial. But Sack's aim is less the achievement of empirical ethnographic accuracy than contrasting primitivity with a distinctively post-primitive modernity. And here the real story begins, with the disruptive events that marked the transformation from primitivity to the civilized and the crucial role that territoriality played in propelling these transformations.

The civilized

What does it mean to be civilized or to speak of a social system as bearing the marks of civilization? In Sack's model being civilized means inhabiting a larger, more impersonal, more stratified political economic system than the primitives do. Following a hypothetical model of the processes by which civilizations emerged *in situ* (in contrast with the processes by which "civilization" arrived from outside and was imposed on indigenous peoples), Sack asks us to imagine a cluster of autonomous but related primitive communities engaged in trade with each other. Over time the different communities begin to specialize in the production of certain trade items. Although there are a number of theories explaining the imagined increase in production in these still primitive trade economies, a central event for Sack is the emergence of a priestly class and the resultant social stratification. The priests, or their agents, take control of the surplus production and manage its storage, distribution, and consumption. This hastens the decline of the more or less reciprocal egalitarianism characteristic of primitive communities. From here the civilization process can take on its own momentum or logic. And this can follow a number of different trajectories. The principal elements of the process are an increased centralization of authority (perhaps localized in a proto-city), urbanization, the emergence and solidification of a class of merchants and traders, and finally, the domination of the satellite communities by the center. Territoriality now becomes significant in the "administration" of tribute areas, and this results in the emergence of recognizable state structures of governance. Administrative districts and their associated authorities are imposed on peasant producers and local communities. With civilization also comes a sort of vertical territoriality. The important point about this intermediate stage of social organization, for Sack's theory, is that the transformations in the history of territoriality are inseparable from the changes in the history of power, particularly the increased significance of impersonal power relations. Implied in this model, but not explicitly addressed, are concomitant changes in communication technologies (writing and literacy) and repressive technologies.

Capitalism

Among the dozens of pre-modern civilizations "only one of them gave rise to capitalism and the modern state" (p. 78). This was the civilization of pre-modern western Europe. What is new and important here is that, with capitalist-riven modernity, we see that

> the repeated and conscious use of territory as an instrument to define, contain and mold a fluid people and dynamic events leads to a sense of an abstract and emptiable space. It makes community seem to be artificial; it makes the future appear geographically as a dynamic relationship between people and events on the one hand and territorial molds on the other. And it makes space seem to be only contingently related to events. (p. 78)

Again the mechanisms of this world-historical transformation are presented in a straightforward way. They are grounded in changes in material conditions, control over production, and the apparatuses of domination. The increasing power of merchants and the gradual proletarianization of labor are the generative processes. Of overriding importance are the means by which producers are forced to participate in the market economy that is controlled by and for the emerging class of capitalists. Sack writes, "One way for merchant capital to take hold is to 'free' peasants from the land so that they can enter into the market while making sure they cannot have the option of returning to subsistence or traditional livelihood if commerce fails" (p. 79).

Over the succeeding generations there came to be an intensified shift from households as the primary unit and locus of production to the creation of factories in which workers no longer had control (ownership) over the means of production (tools) and were increasingly disciplined by a new metrical sense of time. The separation of work and home led, in turn, to a deepening territorial segmentation of most aspects of social life and an increasing significance of hierarchical bureaucratic institutions. This is the story of the rise of the hyper-territorialized life-worlds associated with modernity. Other elements that Sack mentions include the coming into being of the liberal state and its justificatory ideologies of neutrality and freedom; an increase in the mobility of people and things; and the more prominent social role of science and innovative technologies. Science is also associated with a reign of quantification and abstraction which gave rise, in turn, to novel ways of conceiving of space, time, and territory. The geographical extension, through colonialism and imperialism, of political powers located initially in Europe facilitated the virtual globalization of this new social-spatial ordering. Of course, the world was never the same again. Through the political-economic-cultural logic of capitalism there arrived in the world the peculiar territorial logic of modernity that continues to play itself out in various mutations around the world. Of particular importance are the ways in which these distinctively modern conceptions and practices use territory to isolate and aggregate, to empty and fill social space.

This chapter can easily be mistaken as an attempt to accurately capture 7,000 years of collective human experience in a couple of dozen pages. But again, while a certain fidelity to ethnographic and historical facts may be assumed, accuracy is, in a sense, beside the point. Sack's objective is not really to tell us how we arrived at where we are today so much as it is to illustrate aspects of territoriality (or aspects of his theory) as they might be viewed through the thematic lens of change and continuity. The aim is to counter tendencies to isolate territoriality from social processes and from changing social relationships. In a way, it matters little whether the story is accurate (of course it is and of course it couldn't be). It should, rather, be assessed according to its utility for revealing or obscuring what the world is like and how territory might play a role in this.

Case studies

Chapters 4, 5 and 6 of *Human Territoriality* are detailed case studies. Each traces the workings of territory in a specific domain of social life over long periods of time, elucidating the more abstract themes introduced in the first three chapters. Chapter 4 describes significant aspects of territoriality in the long history of institutionalized Christianity, most especially the Roman Catholic Church. Sack discusses early Christian practices as largely continuous with those of Judaism in the time and place of the emergence of Christianity. He shows how the territorial practices changed as the Church became more hierarchical and the power of priests and bishops became more firmly tied to the territorial structure of dioceses and parishes. With the adoption of Christianity by the Roman empire, the territorial structure of the latter served as a template of sorts for the religious-political authority of the Church. Sack touches on the processes through which territoriality was effected by the collapse of the empire, by feudalism and its slow demise, by the Reformation, and, finally, by its more modern bureaucratization.

Chapter 5 concerns transformations in the American political territorial system. This story opens with the story of exploration and discovery, and the dehumanization of indigenous peoples. It proceeds through discussion of colonial expressions of territoriality. Of particular interest are the territorial arguments between the Federalists and anti-Federalists and the ways in which compromises about the territorialization of power came to be constitutionalized. The chapter also includes discussions of westward expansion and contemporary economic interpretations of the territoriality of public good provision. The last substantive chapter is principally concerned with the shifting territoriality of labor – again, from the early modern period to the contemporary era. This discussion, though, also takes into account concurrent changes in the spatial organization of domestic space, "the home," and other distinctively modern institutions such as prisons and the military. Many of the "tendencies" and "combinations" that characterize modern territoriality are clearly exemplified in this chapter.

Beyond Human Territoriality

The value and continued utility of *Human Territoriality* can be seen in a number of features that are unique to it in the literature on territory. Largely unconstrained by scale or by type of territory and largely uncaptured by the more limited concerns of specific disciplines, *Human Territoriality* provides a rich analytic vocabulary that can facilitate our ability to see through territorial practices. Its central concern with the workings of power, its close attention to temporality and historicity, and its emphasis on the significance of material economic forces in combination with its emphasis on conceptual or ideological factors all contribute to the recognition of *Human Territoriality* as a "classic" text of much more than historical value. As a relatively small book, and as an explicitly preliminary effort at that, it is not without its limitations – or boundaries. There are, in *Human Territoriality*, a number of themes that are hinted at but not more fully developed, and a number that are simply of little concern to the author. Some of the absences that are apparent to a reader nearly 20 years later may be the result of Sack's strategy of avoiding capture by narrower disciplinary concerns. For example, there is very little in *Human Territoriality* that directly engages issues of international relations, nationalism, colonialism, gender, racism, or the environment. Moreover, topics and problems that have subsequently emerged as significant were not regarded as such in the 1980s. Among these are border theory, deterritorialization, culture theory, post-modernism, and globalization. Others, such as feminism, were significant then but do not inform the theory or the book's detailed illustrations. Still, reading *Human Territoriality* in light of these other concerns can help us to situate the book vis-à-vis more recent discussions of territory, and thereby reveal its boundaries. In the following pages I will continue the exploration of *Human Territoriality* through engagement with four of these themes: modernity, discourse, identity, and politics. I will then briefly compare *Human Territoriality* with David Sibley's *Geographies of Exclusion* (1995).

Modernity

As we have seen, *Human Territoriality* is very concerned with the theme of modernity. Many of the historical narratives are oriented toward elucidating what is distinctive about modernity vis-à-vis the pre-modern or primitive. The book is very much about the role of territoriality in the process of how we became modern. It also focuses on how territoriality is peculiarly expressed under conditions of modernity: how territoriality undergirds and propels the continual transformations associated with the modern. Especially important for the theory is how territories became conceivable as "emptiable," how modern territorial practices are rooted in cognitive operations of abstraction, and how they give form to impersonal relations. The case is persuasively made that modernity wouldn't – and couldn't – be what it is otherwise.

In the 1980s, when *Human Territoriality* was written, and increasingly throughout the 1990s, the very idea – indeed, the very existence – of modernity was subjected to an unprecedented level of scrutiny (or, as was more often said, "interrogation"). The academic debate that ensued touched all of the human and social disciplines, and, as chapter 2 suggested, this had a pronounced effect on how territoriality was reconsidered. Of course, I cannot even sketch the contours of these wide-ranging conversations, let alone treat the issues with any depth or subtlety. My limited purpose here is simply to recontextualize *Human Territoriality* by way of a contrast with other positions that view the question of modernity differently – and more critically.

In common speech modernity roughly refers to an enduring "now" in contrast to a largely superseded "then." There may be questions about when and how the modern began, or what its defining features are such that, say, Voltaire and George W. Bush are each recognized as being modern but Julius Caesar and Lao Tzu are not. One commonly noted characteristic is that moderns reflect on modernity as a question in ways that primitives or ancients do not (could not) reflect on primitivity or ancientness. Moreover, modern thought can reflect on itself in distinctively modern ways. One common way in which moderns understand modernity is through the celebratory vocabulary of progress and its associated notions of enlightenment, rationality, and freedom. From this perspective, whatever else modernity means it is, on the whole, better than what it replaced, and the processes of modernization and "development" entail a trajectory of overall betterment. Modernity, though, has also spawned a range of critiques ("external" and "internal") that have given greater prominence to the darker aspects of "now" vis-à-vis an actual or imagined "then." Arguably, some versions of post-modern thought, understood as themselves products of modernity, represent the self-critical impulse that some see as one of modernity's greatest achievements. Another way to understand this is to say that "modernity" is not simply a time (an indefinitely expanding "now"), much less a "stage of development" or the ground of progress, so much as it is a disposition, a set of commitments or ideologies and associated practices. According to this view, what is called "modern culture" or "the modern world," while undoubtedly novel, is simply one cultural formation among others. What makes us modern is how we imagine ourselves vis-à-vis *others*. These "others," though, are not only temporal others who are consigned to a rapidly receding past, but cultural others whose annihilation is justified by self-affirming discourses of modernization, progress, and development. Contemporary critiques of modernity, broadly if not quite accurately subsumed under the rubric "post-modernism," often aim to bring these justificatory strategies to light. It should be stressed that the emergence of self-styled *post*-modernist thought in no way entails "the end" of modernity and its replacement by something else, something *after*. If modernity means anything, it is still a going concern and the criticisms launched by post-modernists have not been sufficient to cause its demise. If we regard modernity less as a "fact" about time and more as a way of narrating or representing the history of power – that is, as a story that some moderns are pleased to tell themselves about themselves – then other questions arise that may affect our understanding of territoriality and of *Human Territoriality*.

Robert Sack is explicit in his rejection of the celebratory story of modernity and progress. On the other hand, this repudiation results from a firm commitment to value-neutral social inquiry. This, it might be argued, is a distinctively modernist perspective on the task (and value) of producing knowledge and representations of the social world. The value of value-neutrality is predicated on a particular image of science and its commitment to "objectivity" and self-effacement in the service of progress. In this regard *Human Territoriality* is a paradigmatic modernist project. This is simply to say that an author more skeptical of the facticity of modernity would not have undertaken the project, would not have imagined that territoriality would – or could – have *a* theory or *a single* history. She would be wary of a strategy that reduced 7,000 years of human time and extreme cultural variability to a small set of "mechanisms" presented in the course of 30 pages of a book. Even so, she would most likely not have approached the topic analytically, breaking the vastness of human territoriality into a small number of "causes" (reasons) and "effects" (or consequences). Use of "ideal types" and abstract "models" would be avoided, as would grids of "tendencies" and "combinations." A post- (or other than) modernist theorist would not have so rigorously maintained the neutral, seemingly disinterested voice of "the (social) scientist." As was suggested in chapter 2, she would not have seen territories in such rigid in/out; either/or terms but would have given greater prominence to themes of ambiguity, fluidity, liminality, and heterogeneity. It should go without saying that those features a post-modernist critic would most strongly criticize in *Human Territoriality* are precisely the ones that others find most valuable and praiseworthy.

Beyond these arguably stylistic features, another core modernist assumption that strongly informs *Human Territoriality* concerns what people are like. While *Human Territoriality* puts great stress on the differences between the pre-modern and the modern, one theme of continuity across this divide is the central assumption that the controlling agent (that is, the deployer of territoriality) is a rational, calculating, instrumentally oriented actor. In the very definition of territoriality it is identified primarily as a strategy, a means toward an end. As with any other instrument, territoriality has certain advantages and disadvantages. On the one hand, it is significant that Sack does not use the pre-modern/modern distinction as a surrogate for an irrational (savage)/rational distinction. Indeed, "magical" effects of territoriality are as likely to be identified in the present as in the past. On the other hand, one might regard the *a priori* assumption of rationality as itself mythic. Although Sack himself rejects this interpretation, it is a fact that privileging rationality is a characteristic modernist gesture. In any case, it is not entirely obvious that a calculating rationality is the best key for unlocking the secrets of territoriality, modern or otherwise. Humans "then" as "now" may indeed be capable of rational calculation (I am pleased to believe that I am), and this disposition toward reality is undoubtedly celebrated in modern cultures. But we are also more and other than that. We are often irrational, a-rational, and affective. Territoriality, then, may be much more than "a strategy to control." Territorial practices of all kinds may be more accurately interpreted in terms of desire, fear, disgust, confusion, the will to power, cruelty, or even the workings of "the id." The point is that complicating the implicit view of personhood or the self would entail complicating the theory of territoriality.

Also, assessment of the rationality of *ends* may or may not be separable from assessment of the rationality of *means*. The territorial architecture of the Holocaust can easily be read as employing supremely rational means in service of deeply irrational ends. Giving more attention to the pervasiveness of the other-than-rational in human social relations would facilitate seeing the irrational in the territorialization of nationalism, private property, refugee containment, and even (if not especially) Goffmanesque "territories of the self." One might also read the distinctiveness of modern territoriality as a symptom of the sort of madness that calls itself "rationality." Throughout *Human Territoriality* a key term used in assessments of the advantages and disadvantages of using territoriality as a strategy is "efficiency." An approach to territoriality that was less committed to the modernist story might decenter the themes of efficiency, order, and certainty and put greater emphasis on elements of chaos, ambiguity, or schizophrenia.

Territories, for Sack, are discretely bounded spaces. The most prevalent illustrations in the book are spaces such as fenced fields, rooms, administrative districts, land grants, work stations, and the like. But boundaries and boundedness are, generally speaking, simply taken for granted. In comparison to recent work in border theory, boundaries themselves are relatively unproblematic. "Classification by area" presents territory – in terms of the controller's intentions – as a strongly either/or state of affairs. Again as we saw in chapter 2, more recent theorizing has attempted to deconstruct the stories that controlling territorializers tell about themselves and to supplant them with different stories that reveal the permeabilities and shifting overlaps that characterize territoriality.

For example, Sack's theory tends to reinforce the view of the US–Mexico border as expressing a clearly classifying, clearly communicated line separating distinct sovereign spaces. Moreover, "enforcement," the third of the three most fundamental tendencies, is more problematic. These sovereign territories, as modern territories, exhibit the characteristics of imagined emptiability, abstraction, impersonal relations, and so on. This view is certainly not inaccurate, but neither is it entirely accurate. As was touched on in chapter 2, many others have read this particular example in strikingly different terms: not in terms of mutually exclusive and mutually constitutive "in" and "out" or "either/or," but more in terms of "both/and" – as complexly interpenetrating and fluid. That border, and other boundaries as well, are not merely devices for classifying and separating in any simple sense, but also for constituting and combining at the same time. As Victor Ortiz writes in "The Unbearable Ambiguity of the Border",

> The border region is neither country ... it is not even a country in itself. It is a sociopolitical landscape of dramatic historic and economic dynamics defined by a pervasive dislocation, which is experienced very differently by the individuals and institutions involved. Due to these pervasive contrasts and inequalities, a persistent ambiguity permeates most of its interactions and demarcations ... [the] constant challenging and reinforcing of boundaries generates the contradictory perception of the border region at once as a linking area and a dividing zone under increasingly militarized intervention. As such, the border region is little more than a contested territory, a frontier. (Ortiz 2001, 98)

From this perspective, the point of view that Sack tends to assume can appear to be more a version of the controller's story. But there is always more to the story, and there is always more than one story.

Another basic element of the theory of territoriality is "communication," and more specifically, communication by boundary. Perhaps the prototype – as suggested by many of Sack's examples, is a sign (oral or written) saying "Keep Out" (with the implicit rider "or else"). One here imagines a model of communication that includes a sender (the classifier/controller), a receiver (the controlled), and a clear message (keep out). Under conditions of modernity this communicative event is as likely to be impersonal (directed at "all the world") as personal. But, one might argue, there may be more – much more – to the meanings of territories, boundaries, and power than these relatively transparent commands might suggest. Perspectives on territory that are less modernist might question the accuracy of this transparent communication model and supplement it with greater attention to questions of discourse and the discursivity of territory. I will turn to this theme below.

Again, it should be stressed that setting out these possible contrasts does not in itself constitute a critique of *Human Territoriality*. Neither am I endorsing an other-than-modern perspective. In fact, in perfectly post-modern fashion, one could offer a reading of *Human Territoriality* as itself a (proto)-post-modernist text. The rejection of the celebratory narrative of progress and modernity, the value-neutrality that could be understood as endorsing a kind of relativism, the emphasis on verticality, and the commitment to interdisciplinarity would all help to make this kind of sense of the book. Ultimately, though, such a reading would not do justice to either the achievements of *Human Territoriality* or the utility of post-modernist dispositions.

One last note on the issue of modernity. It is commonly said that the modern/post-modern divide is not simply a matter of academic or es-thetic disposition, but, like the pre-modern/modern divide that serves as its template, it marks a rupture and signifies the emergence of a new kind of world. In this world intensified globalization, de-territorialization, the collapse of the East/West rivalry for world domination, the cyber-revolution, and so on have produced manifestations and "tendencies" of territoriality that were not anticipated by Sack in the 1980s.

Discourse

In the years since *Human Territoriality* was published there has occurred a significant refocusing of attention in social theory and geographical understandings of territoriality toward themes of discourse and representation. In *Human Territoriality* related issues are framed in terms of ideology and, more broadly, "conceptions." As discussed in chapter 2, discourse refers more to large-scale, cultural-cognitive formations and linguistic structures into which social actors are socialized, and which condition thought or consciousness and practice in particular ways. Discourses are not simply collections of beliefs or even ideologies. They are conceptual fields through which difference and sameness are registered. They may not even be articulated, but, rather, may be performed or enacted. Discourses, as ways of thinking and saying, are said to circulate within social orders. They may be closely associated with the production of knowledge and the expert authority to name – to make official sense of social realities. Particular discourses emerge out of and sustain power relations, but they may also weaken or otherwise modify the ways in which power operates. They may be justificatory or critical, naturalizing or denaturalizing. Attention to discourse or discursivity tends to decenter individual intentionality (or, at least, to recontextualize it) and, for our present purposes, put communicative actions or events in a different light.

There are two aspects of discourse analysis that should be noted in a Short Introduction to territoriality: first, there are discourses that take elements of the social as their primary objects and in accordance with which territorial entities are constructed and navigated. Second, there are narrower discourses about territoriality as such. With respect to the former, there are countless discourses through which the social world is comprehended. Some may be regarded as having more general significance than others. What is important is, first, how they are put together: what their most pertinent constitutive distinctions, habitual framings, exclusions, and conceptual hierarchies are; and second, how they are put into play in social practice. Discourses of the social are not inert. They change and are heterogenous. Crucially, they can combine with, reinforce, or challenge one another. Some discourses may emerge as "dominant" or "hegemonic" and take on the appearance of common sense. These last, along with those which directly challenge them, are particularly significant for understanding territoriality. Indeed, much of human territoriality can be understood as a technique through which discourses of differential identities are "inscribed" onto segments of the material world.

For example, in the preceding section I introduced the idea that "modernity" may be less a distinctive historical time than it is a complex narrative (that is, a discourse), albeit one that emerged at a particular time and place and has changed dramatically over time. Among the key constitutive elements of this discourse are the fundamental distinctiveness of "the modern" vis-à-vis the pre-modern (whether this is figured as "primitive" or "ancient"); the story of progress and its companion notions of freedom and rationality; the valorization of the individual subject; the normative priority given to efficiency; and the subsidiary discourses of nature that inform scientism. In some times and places discourses of modernity have combined with discourses of race and sexuality to make narrative sense of colonialism and other forms of domination. In other contexts they have played a role in resisting racial domination. They may combine with discourses of liberalism as easily as with those of socialism. The immediate point is that the discourses of modernity *and their practical deployment* may have profound effects on the processes of territorial inscription. Territoriality can be of fundamental significance to how these discourses can be enacted in the world.

For example, heterosexual masculinity can be territorialized in a number of ways. Consider Lyman and Scott's discussion of gay bars mentioned in chapter 2. They noted that "The style of dress and language among patrons at a bar may immediately communicate to a homosexual that he has arrived in home territory" (1967, 240). But elsewhere this style of dress and language may immediately communicate to others that he is out of place, out of bounds, or out of line. These others may then justify violence against him by reliance on homophobic conceptions of masculinity (Herek and Berrill 1992; Kantor 1998). Likewise, race may be territorialized not only by posting "Whites Only" signs or by forcibly expelling people from spaces but, more subtly, through adherence to "customary" codes of racial etiquette enacted through patterned behaviors of submission or deference.

In chapter 2 we encountered reference to discourses of sovereignty, nationalism, colonialism and anti-colonialism, culture, self, and privacy. One may easily reflect on the profound influence that discourses of race have had on the configuration of territory throughout the world. Of course, the very idea of "race" is historically contingent and, in some accounts, may be better seen not as a justification of colonialism but as one of its effects. Particular historical discursive formations include the scientific racism of the nineteenth and twentieth centuries, in which science was used to naturalize racism, normalize white supremacy, and justify policies of exclusion and genocide. Prevalent racial discourses are very different in the early twenty-first century, and the work they do in shaping territory is also different. Likewise, discourses of gender and sexuality profoundly condition historical and contemporary territorial configurations, particularly when combined with the public/private distinction. And again, discourses of race may not be easily separated from discourses of sexuality, and these might combine in different ways with discourses of rights and liberalism to structure territorial configurations in very complex ways.

For example, historical narratives of race that situate "the races" along a continuum of relative "maturity" were commonly used to justify dispossession, domination, segregation, and exclusion. In some contexts, these discourses combined with discourses of sexuality to support the paired images of the over-sexed and immature black male and the pure and vulnerable white woman, to justify racial subordination. More importantly for our purposes, they provided the justificatory foundation for the hyper-territorialization of race and gender. But they typically combined very differently with respect to white men and black women, such that black women were much more vulnerable to sexual assault by white men, and white men were not liable to be lynched for transgressing racial-gender boundaries. Also, the ways in which discourses of race and sexuality played a role in social territorializations undoubtedly varied in different contexts, say, in the American South or in South Africa, in 1910 or in 1960. These territorializations of power along the axes of race and sexuality were constituted or made intelligible through discourses of power that formed the broader context for specific "strategies" to control or specific acts of "classification," "communication," and "enforcement."

Greater attention to discourse and discursive practices, therefore, would complicate the (more or less) transparent model of communication that informs the theory in *Human Territoriality*. It complicates our understanding of how territorializations give expression to the relationships between power, meaning, and experience. Attending to discourse in this sense allows us to regard territorial complexes – such as those through which race and gender are expressed – more in terms of their cultural and historical particularities, and to situate specific practices, such as segregation, deportation, eviction, or confinement, less in terms of intentional strategies of rational actors and more in terms of cultural performances.

More specifically still, not only does the swirl of social discourses profoundly condition the workings of territoriality, but also specific territorial discourses themselves may recursively inform these social discourses. Here Sack's emphasis on the abstract quality of modern (or perhaps more accurately, literate) cultures is significant. As we saw in chapter 2, discourses of sovereignty, private property, and the self are all made intelligible by reliance on a particular vision of territory as demarcating rather sharply divided "inside/outside" structures onto social space.

Identities

Under the impetus of feminist theories, post-colonial theory, critical race theory, queer theory, culture theory, and other recent academic projects, questions of identity have also undergone significantly greater scrutiny since the publication of *Human Territoriality*. Much of this is connected to the rethinking of territoriality that was discussed in chapter 2. As I suggested above, dominant understandings of identity may be undergirded by conventional discourses of territory. Challenges to these dominant understandings have been advanced through critiques of the conventional discourses of territory which assume an isomorphic relationship between identity and territory. This is most obvious in connection with nationalism. *Human Territoriality* barely touches on this concern. Identity is, at best, simply assumed (there are insiders and outsiders) and the problems relating to identity, difference, sameness, and hierarchy play almost no role in the theory. One of the hallmarks of modern territoriality, for Sack, is the prominence of territorial definitions of social relations (or, perhaps, "membership"). And while this is no doubt an accurate generalization as far as it goes, too strong an emphasis on this can obscure aspects of complexity, heterogeneity, and slippage related to the processes of identity formation and ascription. It therefore allows only a partial view of the role that territoriality plays in these processes.

Dominant territorial discourses, such as those centered on nationalism, tend to treat identity in strongly essentialist terms: "we" simply *are* who we are and "they" are obviously not "us." Likewise, race, sexuality, and gender simply are natural, discrete, enduring categories. Territorial practices are commonly rhetorically oriented toward achieving the proper match between identities (differences) and borders. In order for "outsiders" to be excluded we already have to know who they are and who we are. But, as suggested above, if we come to understand many aspects of identity as not reflecting objective, stable, eternal "facts" but rather as discursively created, revised, and negotiated constructs, we would come to see their relationship to territories differently. The problem of identity is closely related to the theme of discursivity. In an article entitled "Territorial Identities as Social Constructs," political geographer Anssi Paasi argues that scholars should pay closer attention to "the practices and discourses through which the narratives, symbols and institutions of national identity are created and how they become 'sediments' of everyday life, the ultimate basis on which collective forms of identity and territoriality are reproduced" (Paasi 2000a, 93). Situating the politics of identity within the context of globalization, he asks, "How should 'identity' be understood in the contemporary world of flows, where not only ideas and goods move but also human beings, and where interaction between people living in diaspora is becoming easier because of the development of new technologies?"

Wilson and Donnan mention "a new politics of identity, in which the definitions of citizenship, nation and state vie with identities which have acquired a new political significance, such as gender, sexuality, ethnicity and race, among others, for control of the popular and scholarly imaginations of the contemporary world" (1999, 1). This politics has direct effects on how territory, and most especially borders, is understood. "Because of their liminal and frequently contested nature, borders tend to be characterized by identities which are shifting and multiple, in ways which are framed by the specific state configurations which encompass them and within which people must attribute meaning to their experience of border life . . . [T]his is true not only of national identity, but also of other identities such as ethnicity, class, gender and sexualities, identities often constructed at borders in ways which are different from, and shed light on, how these identities are constructed elsewhere in the state" (p. 13).

Discussions such as these focus on the fragmentation or fluidity of national identities in an allegedly globalizing, de-territorializing world of flows, and the problems that this creates for the isomorphic linking of national identities to political territories. But there are many other aspects or ingredients of collective and personal identities (imposed or self-ascribed) that problematize other taken-for-granted assumptions about territory. Again, race and gender provide useful illustrations. In United States history the hyper-territorialization of race was organized, in part, by reference to "the one drop rule" by which "one drop" of what was called "negro blood" (that is, one African ancestor, however remote in time) resulted in the categorization of a person as "a Negro" and so, by definition "not white." Therefore, formally, all of the exclusions, disadvantages, and advantages that accrued to "Negroes," once attached, would be eternal for all of one's descendants, even if they were to all appearances "Caucasians." Hybrid categories such as "mulatto" or "octaroon" or "mixedblood" through which race in America was sometimes made intelligible in social discourses were effaced by the exclusive legal categories of "Negro" and "Caucasian," and these were regulated by the one drop rule. In response to this, some people who were able to made the life-transforming decision to "pass" for white. They were able to escape the confining territorializations of white supremacy. Race is only one among several socially inscribed identities. As we are differentially "raced," so we are differentially "gendered," "aged," and so on. The phenomena of "passing" can be found along these other axes of power as well. To the extent that these lines of power are territorialized, "passing" (or not) or being "outed," having one's cover blown, may be profoundly implicated in how territoriality is experienced. Problematizing "identity" in this way draws our attention to other ways of navigating and negotiating territory. It allows us to see territorial practices as involving more than the practices of classification, communication, and enforcement that are at the heart of Sack's model.

Then there are the countless other identities that are at least partly grounded in the practical workings of territory: the refugee, the native, the tenant, the prisoner, the guard, the fugitive, the occupier, the foreigner, the manager, and so on. These too collide and combine with, or diverge from, the broader and seemingly "inescapable" social categories of nationality, race, gender, and age. To the extent that identity is now regarded as kaleidoscopic, so the territorial elements that take the apparent significance of identity for granted (as more or less fixed by territory) are open to question. Identity in this sense is not a prominent concern of *Human Territoriality*. Once it becomes problematized, so must our understanding of territoriality. In the next chapter we will examine the complex relationship between territoriality and the construction of the identities of "Israeli" and "Palestinian."

Politics

The themes of identity, discourse, and post-modernity were not as prevalent in academic discussions of territory when *Human Territoriality* was written. And even if they had been, their relative absence from Sack's theory would not necessarily have constituted a deficiency. On the other hand, one might have expected the theme of politics to have been given much more prominence. This is especially so given Sack's home discipline of geography: "territory" was virtually owned by political geographers for generations. Sack's account firmly locates the workings of territoriality with those who have or aspire to power over others. But ultimately his is a rather thin reading of power, and "politics" by any definition is almost entirely absent. Having said this, though, one must take note of the fact that the kinds of events, relationships, and practices that are now routinely understood as "political" are somewhat different than those which commonly counted as politics a generation ago.

As we saw in chapter 2, the notion of "the political" may itself be delimited by *a priori* assumptions about territory. Conventional "realist" international relations theory, for example, finds "the political" only within, and not between or among, sovereign states. Other conventional views associate the political with contests for the control of the state or with the procedures and practices of democracy. Again, under the influence of critical theories such as feminism, Marxism, post-structuralism, and critical race theory, "the political" is now recognized as existing within virtually all aspects of social life. Therefore, it may be identified in connection with virtually any territorializing event. Indeed, withholding the term "political" from the workings of social relationships may itself be understood as a tactical depoliticization, that is, as itself a political operation. So if "the political" is everywhere and if it is a non-expungeable element of (possibly) any territorial event, what would it mean to read *Human Territoriality* more politically? As with the topics of modernity, discourse, and identity I can only offer suggestions here. My objective is simply to indicate some of the boundaries of Sack's territory.

First, what is it to be "political"? Any relationship that is infused with power can be thought of as implicating a kind of politics. Politics names all of the social activities and events surrounding social relationships characterized by domination, subordination, contestation, resistance, co-operation, solidarity, accommodation, or negotiation. This is no less true for gender relations, race relations, relations between young people and authorities, or workplace relationships than for relations between governments or between state actors and non-state actors. Accordingly, any expression of territoriality (for example, the imposition of territorial grids on indigenous peoples, the exclusion of children from rooms, the confinement of refugees to camps, the eviction of squatters from buildings, the exclusion of women from country clubs) will have a political dimension to it. Reciprocally, many forms of political action (the politics of identity, the politics of social movements, gender politics, environmental politics) will implicate territory in complex ways. To the extent that power infuses social relationships, so must politics. Part of the point of discourse analysis is to reveal the politics attendant on putatively apolitical events, to uncover both the justificatory ideologies and the counter-ideologies through which elements of the world are made meaningful. For all of its considerable virtues *Human Territoriality* takes the perspective of those who would impose their will on (control) others. There is very little interest in either what it is like to be on the receiving end of attempts to control or how the dynamics of resistance or evasion affect territorializing processes. Generally speaking, for Sack, the controlled either submit or are punished. This gives a very skewed sense of how territoriality actually works in the world. To that extent it gives a skewed sense of how social worlds are created, revised, and maintained through territoriality.

Relatedly, expunged from the numerous examples and illustrations provided in *Human Territoriality* is any acknowledgment of the role that violence plays in territorializing practices. The commands of the controllers may be "enforced," transgressors may be "punished," but these words tend to sanitize the territorial configurations in question. Thus, in chapter 1 of *Human Territoriality* the transformations at work in Chippewa territories show no trace of the violence and suffering that they entailed. Likewise, the transformations attendant on the emergence and maintenance of capitalism are described like this: "One way for merchant capital to take hold is to 'free' peasants from the land so that they can enter into the market while making sure they cannot have the option of returning to subsistence or traditional livelihood if commerce fails" (p. 79). How did they "make sure"? How did the peasants respond to being "freed" from the option of feeding themselves? Many, perhaps most, manifestations of territoriality are not occasioned by the direct use of violence, but many, perhaps most, entail at least the implied threat if "the controllers" do not get their way. Sovereignty and private property – the foundational pillars of much of modern territoriality – are themselves anchored in the play of violence and fear. *Human Territoriality*, therefore, is a rather bloodless account of what is often a very messy and emotionally volatile aspect of human socio-spatial organization. Had Sack looked more closely at the other side of territorial relationships, he might have identified other significant tendencies and combinations.

Other ways of seeing through territory

The aim here is simply to re-examine the boundaries of *Human Territoriality* so as to reveal some of what is excluded or marginalized from that perspective. To this end it may be useful to briefly compare Sack's book to David Sibley's *Geographies of Exclusion* (1995). Sibley's book is not a theoretical excursion through the territory of territoriality as such. Nor does Sibley aspire to Sack's broad historical sweep. And while the book is written from a "post-disciplinary" perspective (p. xv), it is essentially a social geography that is informed by psychoanalysis and an ethnography of the ordinary. Sibley's primary concern is with the spatial aspects of interpersonal relationships as these are structured by discourses of difference. Especially important for Sibley are discourses of race, gender, and age and the roles they play in "the discursive production of outsiders" (p. xv). The most significant feature of what we have been calling territoriality, for Sibley, is how it functions in the social processes of marginalization and oppression. He defines "social control" in terms that are similar to those of Sack: "Social control...is the attempted regulation of behaviour of individuals and groups by other individuals or groups in dominant positions" (p. 81). But, in contrast to Sack – and most other theorists – Sibley's starting point is with the experiential aspects of territory. "I want to start," he writes, "by considering people's feelings about others because of the importance of feelings in their effect on social interaction, particularly in instances of racism and other forms of oppression" (p. 3). His guiding questions are also strikingly different. He asks, "who are places for? whom do they exclude? and how are these prohibitions maintained in practice? Apart from examining legal systems and the practices of social control agencies, explanations of exclusion require an account of barriers, prohibitions and constraints on activities from the point of view of the excluded" (p. x). Of special interest is understanding "how the processes of control are manifested in the exclusion of those people who are judged to be deviant, imperfect or marginal [and]...processes of boundary erection by groups in society who consider themselves to be normal or mainstream" (p. xv). Among these processes are those that are involved in working out the terms of "abjection" and "purification." Abjection is "the key to an understanding of exclusion" (p. 11). "[T]he urge to make separations, between clean and dirty, ordered and disordered, 'us' and 'them', that is, to expel the abject, is encouraged in western cultures, creating feelings of anxiety because such separations can never be fully achieved" (p. 8). And, "Separation is a part of the process of purification – it is the means by which defilement or pollution is avoided – but to separate presumes a categorization of things as pure and defiled" (p. 37).

Sibley's reading of territoriality in the modern home provides a stark counterpoint to Sack's. Acknowledging that " 'The house as haven' is a much more common theme [in social science] than 'the house as source of conflict' " (p. 92), he nonetheless focuses attention on the workings of territory, power, and experience within at least some homes. "[W]here the desire for a purified environment is not shared by all members of a household, the home is a place of conflict" (p. 91). "In the domestic sphere, dominant individuals would be concerned with the maintenance of spatial boundaries, keeping children out of adult spaces, for example, and with the temporal regulation of children's activities. Keeping control means maintaining clear, unambiguous boundaries" (p. 96). Linking these territories to wider social forces, Sibley speculates that

> Constant exclusion and rigid boundary enforcement or persistent intrusion into the lives and living spaces of children may...contribute to behaviour problems in children and adolescents...The home which is projected as a highly ordered and unpolluted space by purveyors of home furnishings does not provide a sympathetic environment for children. Exclusionary tendencies are exacerbated by commercial representations of ideal homes which render children a polluting presence. (p. 98)

David Sibley's significantly darker view of the possible operations of territoriality in the modern home arises from his empathy with the excluded, marginalized, and defiled. Territory, and our hyper-territorialized life-worlds, look and feel differently from this point of view. Indeed this point of view is itself commonly excluded from explorations of territoriality. The point, though, is not that Sibley's view is correct or that Sack's stands in need of correction. Each is necessarily incomplete. *Geographies of Exclusion* has the value of demarcating some of the boundaries of *Human Territoriality*. And reading *Human Territoriality* in light of *Geographies of Exclusion* reveals "tendencies" in addition to those that Sack enumerated. Such a reading also complicates the commitment to rationalism that informs much of *Human Territoriality*, and indeed, foregrounds elements of social pathology that infuse distinctively modern territorial configurations at all scales.

4

Parsing Palisraelestine

Introduction

"Danger. Military Area. Anyone crossing or touching the fence does so at his own risk," is written on the sign over the fence. The latest innovation of the occupation, these yellow iron gates – the locked transit points of the separation fence which, in this area, separates farmers from their fields. This is a "humanitarian" arrangement that will last, one may venture to guess, a very brief time, pursuant to which Border Police come periodically to open the gate for caged-in farmers, a good will gesture from the most humane military force in the world. (Levy 2003)

The objective of this chapter is to examine many of the themes presented so far in this Short Introduction within a more sustained empirical context. For this purpose the choice of Israel/Palestine may seem foolhardy, not least because of the volatility of the situation. Facts on the ground may well be very different by the time this book is published. Additionally, because there is little resembling a consensus on how to assess these facts and because, for many, this is an extremely emotion-laden situation, my task is certainly complicated. On the other hand, as Israeli geographer David Newman has recently written,

There are few better live laboratories for the study of political geography and attempts at conflict resolution than Israel/Palestine. It involves the study of territory and territorial change at several levels from attempts to demarcate national boundaries between states, to control ownership of resources (land, settlements, water) through residential segregation of Jews and Arabs in their exclusive, monoethnic settlements and neighborhoods...Importantly...it shows how important the territorial dimension remains for understanding the political organization of space, even in this "borderless and deterritorialized" world and smallest of territories. (2002, 632)

As argued in chapter 1, part of how ideas and practices of territoriality are supposed to work is through the communicative processes of clarification and simplification. I suggested there that scholarship should instead seek to see through territoriality to reveal its hidden complexities and ambiguities – or rather, the complexities and ambiguities that it helps to hide. The workings of territoriality in the land of Israel/Palestine are nothing if not complex and ambiguous. As already noted, the topic (and the experiences gathered together under the name of the topic) are deeply contentious. It is reasonable to ask whether such a situation can be analyzed dispassionately from a distance. I think that one can answer yes while acknowledging that no analysis is immune from critique. Already, simply by identifying the location as "Israel/Palestine" instead of "Israel" or "Palestine" or "Palestine/Israel" or perhaps "Palisraelestine," because it is a choice, can be criticized as the wrong place to start. One indisputable fact about the situation – and this also argues in favor of it as an appropriate one in which to study the unfoldings of territoriality – is the profound human tragedies with which it is so tightly bound. This is no antiseptic story about "power" in the abstract. The violence with which territoriality is imposed and resisted and the suffering that is engendered are palpable. If nothing else the violent territorializations and re-territorializations of Israel/Palestine – whether accomplished through suicide bombs in cafés or bulldozers in refugee camps – highlight why territory matters.

Given the complexities of the facts and the various perspectives on these facts, and given the limited scope of this Short Introduction, what follows will, of necessity, be somewhat cursory. This is not a book about Israel/Palestine; it is a book about territory. My immediate and limited aim is to provide a more sustained illustration of some of the principal themes we have already encountered, not to provide a comprehensive feel for the situation as a whole. I will trace how forms of power find expression through territoriality and how territoriality conditions how lives are lived. I will emphasize aspects of the unfolding of territorial complexes through time, not as disembodied mechanisms but as conditions and effects of situated actors making their worlds of experience meaningful. The focus will not be on territories as discrete containers but as components of complex, fluid constellations. The initial sections present a rough sketch of a genealogy of territory in a manner not unlike Sack's more extended illustrations. Here I touch on major elements of the constellation and key episodes or re-territorializations. This will be followed by a somewhat more detailed – but still quite general – survey of the transformations in land tenure and property relations as key components of the larger constellation. Important here are the projects and practices related to the "Judaization" of territory within "Israel proper" and, after 1967, within the "Occupied Territories." Next I present a more synchronic survey of some of the most significant components of what has been called the "Israeli System of Control" (Kimmerling 1989) and what I will refer to as the Israeli *Territorial* System of Control. This is a device through which power – especially, but not exclusively, physical force – is circulated, distributed, and experienced. Among the components of this system are refugee camps, Jewish settlements in the Occupied Territories, and devices of immobilization such as checkpoints, curfews, and graduated "closures." The most recent addition to this territorial system is a barrier wall that is being constructed within the Occupied Territories to separate (some) Israelis from (most) Palestinians. After these elements are presented I will discuss the territoriality of contemporary Israel/Palestine in terms of some of the principal themes of the book.

The method that I use to present this sketch is to draw extensively, if not exclusively, on the words of Israeli and Jewish historians, geographers, anthropologists, sociologists, architects, legal scholars, human rights activists, and journalists who have examined elements of the territorial system. These observations and assessments are particularly significant not only because these are some of the people on whose behalf and in whose name the system has been constructed and maintained but also because these voices provide evidence of an internal critique of the Israeli territorial project. That is to say, it requires that we distinguish between those Israelis who support the effects of the system and those who oppose these effects and would advocate other ways of territorializing power in this part of the world. Their words should therefore be read not only as those of authoritative experts but as those of participants in a project of reimagining. A fuller description of the Israeli Territorial System of Control would give greater prominence to the justifications of its creators and maintainers. These would refer to the right, need, and duty of the state of Israel to protect its citizens from the atrocities of anti-Israeli violence. (And here one might note that the indiscriminate bombing of civilians by Palestinian militants kills and maims Arabs as easily as Jews.) But such a description could also include arguments that the draconian measures of collective punishment are generative of less rather than more "security." In any case what follows is a description of a territorial complex that was created and is maintained and revised for the purposes of dispossessing, excluding, expelling, and confining Palestinian people.

The Unfolding of Sovereignties

In the nineteenth century, arguably, there was no "Israel" and no "Palestine" – at least as these places are understood now. Certainly there were neither Israelis nor Palestinians. But, arguably, there have been both an Israel and a Palestine for millennia. Of course, in the mid-nineteenth century there were hundreds of thousands of people living and working in the area near the southeastern corner of the Mediterranean Sea between the sea and the Jordan River. Most of these people were Arabic-speaking Muslims, some were Jews, and some were Christian Arabs. Most were peasants engaged in subsistence agriculture and livestock-raising. Some were Bedouins (nomadic herders). Most lived in small villages, some lived in small towns such as Nablus, Hebron, Jerusalem, and Jaffa. The large-scale social structures were organized by clans or extended families and were markedly stratified. In this life-world territoriality was a significant dimension of social life. Complex rules of access conditioned land use and land tenure, village life, home life, and religious practice. Some of this will be described in greater detail later in this chapter.

These experiential spaces of rural, village, and town life were overlaid, so to speak, by the territorialities of political sovereignty and administration. Formally, this part of the world was a relatively peripheral region of the Ottoman empire, which was politically centered in Istanbul. As with other marginal places, the land that would become Israel/Palestine/Jordan was significant for rulers as a source of taxes and conscripts. Direct involvement by central authorities was, by contemporary standards, rather loose (Kimmerling and Migdal 2003). The area was governed through a territorial system of *vilayets* and *sanjaqs*, or administrative districts (see map 1). In 1831 a military operation led by Muhammad Ali resulted in the occupation of much of the area by Egyptians. After the Ottoman empire reasserted control in 1840 the area was regarded by the Ottoman authorities as having greater strategic significance, and the presence of the central state became more noticeable. One expression of this greater involvement was the promulgation of the Ottoman Land Code of 1858, which was an effort to rationalize land tenure. To that extent it can be understood as an intervention in the territoriality of everyday life. At least as significant is that this land law became a sort of sedimentary structure upon which subsequent re-territorializations were to be constructed.

At the same time, other, broader transformations in global political economy and culture were also beginning to have noticeable effects. The introduction of cash crops such as cotton, sesame, and oranges affected

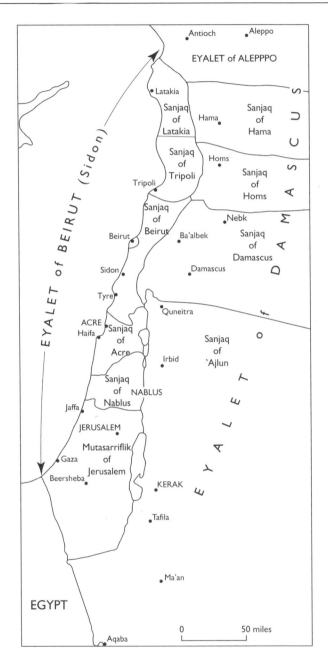

Map 1 *Palestine under Ottoman rule*

Source: Kimmerling and Migdal 2003. Harvard University Press; Cartography Department, Hebrew University. Used with permission

land use and labor and, consequently, patterns of rural subsistence and household economies (Kimmerling and Migdal 2003; Pappe 2004). The emergence of Jerusalem and "the Holy Land" as tourist destinations for Europeans and Americans had the effect that central authorities began to pay still closer attention to the area. But by far the most important factor for the subsequent story of territory was the invention in Europe of Zionism.

Zionism, in its various forms and functions, is an ideology of Jewish nationalism that was developed in late nineteenth-century Europe along with, and in response to, other nationalisms (Dieckhoff 2003). It, and its associated discourses, was an aspirational solution to problems attending what was called "the Jewish Question." Facing, on the one hand, continued persecution in eastern Europe and, on the other, the very different problem of assimilation in western Europe, combined with anti-Semitic racism throughout the diaspora, some Jewish political thinkers such as Theodor Herzl began to articulate a geographical strategy for self-determination. This involved the massive colonization of Jews from throughout the world to, as they called it, Eretz Yisrael, the eternal Jewish homeland. Significantly, as Kimmerling put it in his book-length study *Zionism and Territory*, "During the course of time the concept of Zion became increasingly metaphysical and abstract. Its boundaries were unclear and undefined, except for its center – Jerusalem" (1983, 8–9).

> But, this Zion, abstract as it was (and perhaps partly because of that) became a mobilizing symbol of the Jewish national movement. It became apparent that only Eretz Israel could serve as a powerful enough symbol to recruit significant numbers of the Jewish people throughout the world for collective political, social, and economic activity, either as actual participants in immigration and building a new society, or as moral and/or material supporters of the movement. Other territorial alternatives were suggested (Uganda, northern Sinai, Argentina, and even a Soviet proposal to establish a Jewish Republic in Birobidzhan) which aroused a great amount of controversy in the Zionist movement, but they were all eventually discarded as "non-Zionist." (1983, 9)

The appropriate place of this Zion of the imagination had another important characteristic. As Ghazi-Walid Falah writes, "It is almost impossible to touch upon the land discourse debate in the Israeli/Palestinian conflict without having to remember the Zionist slogan of 'a land without a people for a people with no land' " (2003, 182). This representation was, of course, sharply at odds with reality. It was, at best, wishful thinking, or perhaps the discursive precursor for the actual dispossession and expulsion of the people who were indeed inhabiting this land. "The sobering up came as soon as the mass migration to Zion began in 1882 ... The reality was a far cry from what had been envisaged. There was very little free land available" (Kimmerling 1983, 10). As will be discussed in more detail below, these obstacles (the presence of people and the unavailability of land) may have presented logistical difficulties but they were not regarded as insurmountable. Moreover, that Zion was formally part of the Ottoman empire "was seen only as a legal compli- cation," and that the land was owned by others was simply "a financial problem" that could be solved through fundraising (Kimmerling 1983, 9). The Zionist project for "redeeming" the land of Israel as the homeland of the Jews was to take place simultaneously on two territorial planes, that of sovereignty and that of property, and at their intersection. By 1903, 20 Jewish settlements had been established with a combined population of 10,000 people. (Bickerton and Klausner 1995, 22). A significant amount of financial support was provided by Baron Rothschild.

Baruch Kimmerling contrasts the Jewish settler movement with others, such as settler colonies in North America, by noting that, "in Palestine there was no frontier whatsoever" (1983, 13). But, in a sense, through the strategic location of settlements a kind of de facto "frontier" was brought into being. Israeli political geographer Oren Yiftachel writes,

> For Zionist culture, the "frontier" became a central icon, and its settlement was considered one of the highest achievements. The frontier *kibbutzim* (collective rural villages) provided a model, and the reviving Hebrew language was filled with positive images drawn from religious myths of national redemption such as *aliya lakorka* (literally "ascent to the land," i.e. settlement), *ge'ulat korka* (land redemption), *hityashvut, hitnahalut* (positive Biblical terms for Jewish settlement), *kibbush hasmama* (conquest of the desert), and *hagshama* (literally "fulfillment" but denoting the settlement of the frontier). (2002a, 228)

This discourse of redemption and conquest informed the territorial pro- ject of "Judaization" and was inseparable from the process of identity formation. As Yiftachel writes,

> Ethnic control over space, and the "purification" of this space becomes the primary goal...Seizing and claiming sovereignty over contested space is closely tied with the *denial* of the other claims to that space, that is, the Other's history, place and political aspirations are presented as a menacing package to be thoroughly rejected ... The geographical Judaization program was premised on a hegemonic myth cultivated since the rise of Zionism, and buttressed by the "nation-state" myth that "the land" (Ha'aretz) be- longs to the Jews and only to them. An exclusive ethno-national culture was coded, institutionalized and militarized by the new state, in order to quickly "indigenize" immigrant Jews, and to conceal, trivialize, or margin- alize the land's Palestinian past. (2002a, 227–228)

In terms of the relationship of territoriality to the construction of identity, Yiftachel continues, "the glorification of the frontier was central to the construction of 'the New Jew' – an ever ready settler–fighter who conquers the land with his physical strength and endless poetic love" (2002a, 228). In this mythic space the non-Jewish Palestinians were understood as intruders. Ultimately what was required was the construction of a specifically (Jewish) Israeli identity out of the various ethnic identities (eastern European, western European, Middle Eastern, North African) that had developed in diaspora. However, the disruptive effect on social structure, political power, and, ultimately, everyday experience also provided the foundation for the construction of a distinctive Palestinian identity as colonized, set against that of Jewish (European) colonizers (Farsoun 1997; Khalidi 1997). Kimmerling notes, for example, that, "in July and August 1913, the Arabic newspaper *Palestine* called for the establishment of a patriotic Palestinian organization to be made up of wealthy people from Nablus, Jerusalem, Jaffa, Haifa and Gaza to purchase lands in government possession before the Zionists could do so (Kimmerling and Migdal 2003, 15).

In *Zionism and Territory* Kimmerling presents a model of the Zionist strategy in terms of the interplay among " . . . three types of control over territorial regimes: presence, ownership and sovereignty" (1983, 20). By "presence" in this context he means "the existence of Jewish settlement on any tract of land . . . [and] the consolidation of control over the land by creation of *faits accomplis*" (p. 20). Second, "In the Israeli case, public or institutional ownership . . . played a decisive role, and, in the period before sovereignty, was a substitute for sovereignty because it was only by public ownership that it was possible to freeze the land which had been transferred from Arab to Jewish ownership" (p. 21). Later we will examine the mechanisms of this part of the process in somewhat greater detail. Of monumental significance for the success of this territorial strategy was the establishment of the Jewish National Fund (JNF) in 1901. "The JNF acted to a large extent as the functional equivalent of a sovereign state. The JNF bought land for the same reason that the United States, for example, bought Louisiana from France in 1803 and Alaska from Russia in 1867" (p. 23). Kimmerling's analysis of the territorial strategy is that the

> combination of ownership and presence . . . had special significance . . . Until the Jews acquired sovereignty in 1948 . . . [t]erritories were acquired and settled, and a territorial continuum was formed between them . . . By means of these two types of control, a method of building a nation was developed, based primarily on the acquisition of adjacent tracts of land and creating settlement points on them. This method even became ideologized and was

crystallized into a political movement known as "Practical Zionism." Its motto was "a dunam [approximately a quarter of an acre] here, a dunam there," with the intention of combining all the dunams "here" and "there" into a single territorial tract. (1983, 23–24)

The third type of control, sovereignty, was the desired endpoint. According to Hussein and McKay, "Once land had been purchased, non-Jews were excluded from it and prevented from deriving any benefit from it. Land acquired by the JNF was automatically considered 'redeemed,' and the property of the Jewish people as a whole" (2003, 68). As Palestinian geographer Ghazi-Walid Falah interprets the process,

the purchase of an extra dunam...of land from a Palestinian [was], however minuscule, translated into a patriotic "achievement" by the state and its Jewish citizenry, while simultaneously perceived as treachery in the eyes of the indigenous Palestinians. This kind of dichotomy in perception, a territorializing par excellence of the basic confrontation, accorded the possession of the land an added value in the mind of Jews and Arabs, one far exceeding its economic exchange value: indeed, land (cum water) and its control have become a prime emblem of the conflict, its very signature. (2003, 183)

Consider a particular small tract of land situated, say, in the Jezreel Valley in 1905. Ownership of this tract carried with it much more than a sign saying simply "Keep Out" might signify. It would be understood as a component of a more extensive (and projected) territorial complex. Its significance would be made intelligible with reference to the discourses of Zionism as itself combining elements of nationalism, religious symbolism, response to persecution, and the tragedy of diaspora tied to an international network of fundraising. It would also be made meaningful by reliance on powerful contemporary discourses of colonialism that more easily positioned Jews from Europe as agents of civilization vis-à-vis benighted Arabs. All of this would be experienced more directly in terms of dispossession, exclusion, and frustration.

It is important to keep in mind that even in 1910 the success of the Zionist territorial project was by no means inevitable. The strategy of building a sovereign territory out of "presence" and "ownership" required, first, that presence be maintained against opposition. (And this opposition had already taken the form of violence against Jews.) Second, it required the participation of willing Arab sellers. Third, it required the acquiescence of the state, or, at least, the incapacity or unwillingness of the state to prohibit land transfers. Also, Zionism itself might have remained a rather marginal, inconsequential movement. In the early twentieth century comparatively few European Jews were Zionists and, at least initially, only a minuscule number of Jews who did leave Europe went to Palestine. However, the program did meet with enough local success to achieve, within two generations, transformations of world-historical significance.

This sketch presents elements of the Zionist territorial strategy only in the broadest outline. We will later return to the dynamics of forging sovereign territory out of ownership territory. For the present it is enough simply to emphasize the complex interconnections among ideologies, identities, and territory that are at work here. One significant element of divergent understandings of these interconnections, according to Yiftachel, is that, "whereas the Palestinians saw their collective territorial identity as inclusive (that is, all people residing in Palestine were considered Palestinians, including 'pre-Zionist' Jews), Zionists only regarded Jewish newcomers as part of the nation. Palestinian nationalism was, then, on course to develop incrementally as a modernizing territorial political organization typical to in situ collectivities" (2002a, 225). That is to say, in this reading Palestinians were assuming, in terms of Sack's theory, a more modernist territorial definition of social relations whereas Zionists were assuming a pre-modernist social definition of territory.

Re-territorializing sovereignty

These local territorializing moves were profoundly affected by other territorializing maneuvers originating far away that had, initially, little to do with either Zionism or emerging Palestinian nationalism. In 1914 the area between the Mediterranean Sea and the Persian Gulf was part of the Ottoman empire. The empire was allied with Germany and Austria in World War I. One of the more significant results of that war was the "dismemberment" of the empire. This was a re-territorialization of the greatest magnitude. In its place appeared the nation-state of Turkey and the colonization of most of the non-Turkish parts of the former empire by victorious European powers. Particularly important for subsequent events were the details of the partition of the region by Britain and France.

While the war was still in progress Sir Mark Sykes and Charles François Georges-Picot arranged for the post-war division of the region. There was envisioned a zone in which the French would exercise direct control, a zone of "indirect" French control, a zone of British control, and a zone of "indirect" British control. Much of the land of Palestine would be under joint French and British control (see map 2). However, also during this period the British had been negotiating with Sherif Hussein of Mecca concerning the establishment of an Arab state in Palestine (Bickerton and Klausner 1995, 36–38). Then, in 1917, in what has become

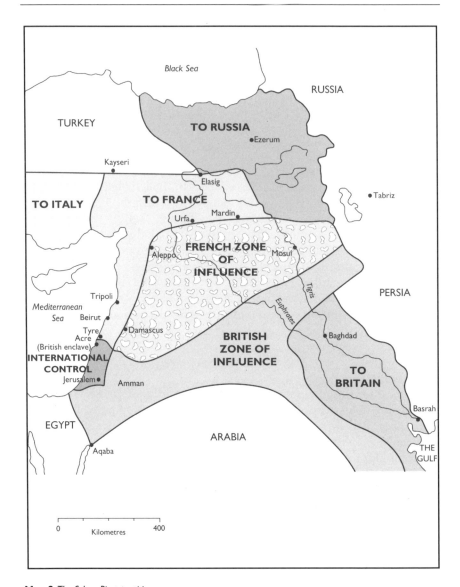

Map 2 *The Sykes–Picot partition*

Source: Anderson 2000. Routledge. Used with permission

known as the Balfour Declaration, the British government announced support for a Jewish homeland in Palestine. Clearly, the re-territorialization of sovereignty here was rife with contradictions and ambiguities at best. In 1920, some of this became clarified in the Treaty of Sèvres. As Bickerton and Klausner put it,

Instead of zones of British and French influence and internationalized areas... the territory was divided into new entities called "mandates." The mandates would be administered by the French and the British, under the supervision of the League of Nations, until such time as the inhabitants were ready for independence and self-government... Wartime pledges and promises to the Arabs and Jews alike were postponed, if not altogether negated by these arrangements. (1995, 42–43)

In effect, what would become in 1943 the nation-states of Syria and Lebanon were "awarded" to France and what would become the nation-state of Iraq in 1932 was "awarded" to Britain, as was Palestine. What had been called "Palestine" then consisted of what is now Israel, the Occupied Territories, and Jordan. In 1921 a new entity called Trans-Jordan was carved off and set up as a separate mandate. "The preamble of the Palestinian Mandate reaffirmed the obligation of Britain to put the Balfour Declaration into effect." The British were to "facilitate Jewish immigration under suitable conditions" and encourage "close settlement by the Jews on the land" (Bickerton and Klausner 1995, 43). And, as Bickerton and Klausner point out, "The Mandate instrument never mentioned the Arabs by name" (p. 43). In short, Palestine now became a British colony and Zionism became official colonial policy. These macro-territorial moves were not simply exercises in imaginative cartography. Through the reconstitution of territorial complexes relations of power were reconfigured, and these lines of power were maintained by the threat and use of violence. Moreover, the deployment of violence by agents of the colonial states called forth counter-violence by both Arabs and Jews.

The Mandate period in Palestine saw profound transformations in all aspects of social life. Economically some areas were more firmly integrated into the grid of international markets through the emphasis on cash crops and industrialization along the coast, while the hilly interior regions were underdeveloped (Kimmerling and Migdal 2003). This uneven "modernization" of Palestine induced a host of other social changes, among them the intensification of stratification within Arab social structures. Meanwhile, on the ground, Zionist land purchases continued at an accelerated pace, as did the formation of various exclusive Jewish institutions and settlements. An increasingly segregated dual society was taking clearer shape. In the period 1936–39 there was a widespread uprising of Arabs against both the continued immigration of Jews and the transfer of property to Jews. At the outbreak of World War I there had been approximately 60,000 Jewish people living in Palestine (less than 10 percent of the population). They owned 3 percent of the land. By 1939 their numbers had increased to 600,000 (31 percent) and they, largely through the JNF, controlled more than 20 percent of the land (Farsoun 1997). The "Arab Revolt" of 1936–39 was suppressed by the British. Anti-Jewish violence was met by more organized Jewish paramilitary organizations which were themselves legitimated and trained by the British (Pappe 2004). The militarization of social life in Palestine was well under way. In 1939 the British published a "White Paper" which called for restrictions on Jewish immigration and land purchases and declared that Palestine would be independent within 10 years. As there was still an overwhelmingly Arab majority this seemed to suggest that this would be an Arab state with a Jewish minority. However, World War II, the Holocaust, and other local events would all combine to negate this possibility.

The rise of the Third Reich, the beginning of another world war, and the unspeakable depravity of the Holocaust all reinforced the belief that the Jewish people could not be safe without a homeland that could secure the means of self-determination and self-defense. As the close of the previous world war had seen the re-territorialization of Palestine, so did the close of this one. This time the victorious powers agreed upon the establishment of the state of Israel. But there remained the stubborn facts of the existence and location of Palestinian people. They saw no reason why the security of the Jews should be purchased with their rights and aspirations (and on their land). Also, and not incidentally, Syria, Egypt, Lebanon, Jordan, Iraq, and Saudi Arabia were all, by war's end, sovereign states. There was an obvious practical problem and there was a range of territorial solutions presented by others about Arabs and Jews in Israel/Palestine. In 1947 The United Nations negotiated a partition plan for the creation of two convoluted micro-states and an "international" zone around the city of Jerusalem (see map 3). This imaginative re-territorialization had as its foundation the patterns of "presence" and "ownership" that had been built up over the preceding 60 years.

In 1948 all of this became moot and a different set of territorial practices came into play. Against a backdrop of international diplomacy Jewish and Arab paramilitary forces and terrorists became engaged in armed conflict, the former to solidify the position of the soon-to-be-declared state of Israel, the latter to prevent its creation. On May 14, 1948 the Mandate government effectively evaporated and the state of Israel declared its presence among the sovereign states of the world. The next day armed forces from Syria, Iraq, Jordan, Egypt, Lebanon, and Saudi Arabia attacked. The first Arab–Israeli war had begun. Within half a year Israel effectively defeated the combined Arab armies. One result of the war was that Israel was 20 percent larger than it would have been under the UN partition plan. It now occupied nearly 80 percent of Mandate Palestine. The ceasefire line (called the Green Line) became the de facto border of

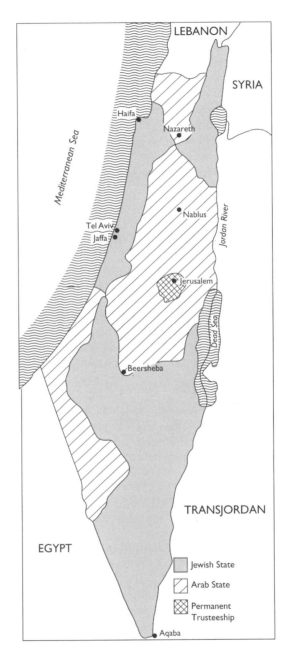

Map 3 *United Nations Recommendation for a two-states solution in Palestine, 1947*

Source: Kimmerling and Migdal 2003. Harvard University Press; Cartography Department, Hebrew University. Used with permission

Israel. The area of Palestine west of the Jordan River that was not under Israeli control (the West Bank) was annexed by Jordan, and the small coastal area around the city of Gaza (the Gaza Strip) was occupied and administered (but not annexed) by Egypt (see map 4). But again, lines on a map are one thing, social reality is often very different. At the outbreak of military hostilities the area that would become Israel was inhabited by 1.6 million people. Of these 30 percent were Jews and nearly 70 percent were Palestinian Arabs. If these relative proportions were to remain then the new sovereign state of Israel might have had difficulties remaining a distinctively Jewish, in contrast to a multi-ethnic, nation. Here again, the solution to this difficulty was reflected in another round of re-territorializations.

After 1948

Among the first acts of sovereignty by the Israeli government was the passage of the Law of Return, which granted automatic citizenship to any Jew immigrating to Israel without having to go through a formal natur-alization process (Davis 1987). But other aspects of the territorial Juda-ization process exemplify some of the tragic dimensions of Sackian "emptiable space" (see chapter 3). The war that Israelis call the War of Independence also resulted in what Palestinians call al-Naqbah ("the Catastrophe").

> More than half of the Arabs of western Palestine became refugees; the community was destroyed. More than 60 percent of Israel's total area, excluding the Negev, was land formally occupied by Palestinians. Further-more, entire cities and towns were taken over by Israel. Jaffa, Acre, Lydda, Ramle, Beit Shean, and Majdal were among these 388 towns and villages. In all, a quarter of all the buildings in Israel (100,000 dwellings, and 10,000 shops, businesses, and stores) were formally Palestinian. (Bickerton and Klausner 1995, 105)

Nearly three-quarters of a million Palestinian people "fled or were driven out of the land by Jewish forces, over 420 Palestinian villages were destroyed" (Yiftachel 2002a, 227). Now "refugees," they were prevented from returning to their homes and villages after armistice agreements with belligerent states were signed. Some of the displaced were able to find sanctuary in neighboring Arab states, but the vast majority were eventually relocated to refugee camps in Lebanon, Jordan, Syria, the West Bank, and Gaza. We will take up their story later.

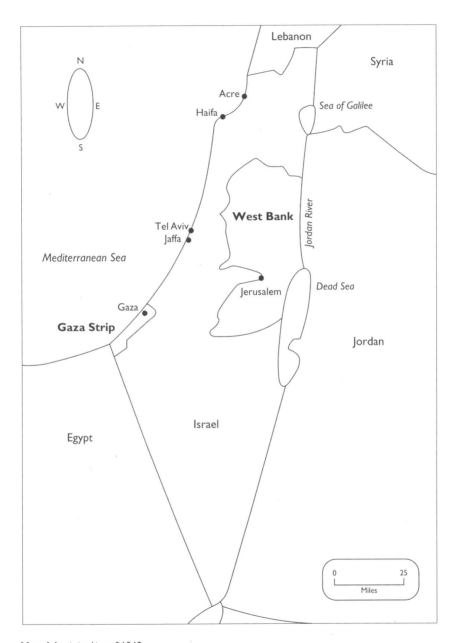

Map 4 *Armistice Line of 1949*

Source: Bornstein 2002b. University of Pennsylvania Press. Used with permission

Approximately 160,000 Palestinians remained in Israel. With respect to these people territoriality was crafted in such a way as to maximize control:

> The Palestinian Arabs in Israel were placed under military rule and forbidden to move outside their areas without permits. They were forbidden to form their own political parties. Under the Defense (Emergency) Regulations imposed, which were not lifted until 1966, military governors had extensive powers over the Palestinians. Arabs could be exiled or arrested and detained without reason; villages and land could be expropriated by declaring an area a "security zone." (Bickerton and Klausner 1995, 106)

The details of the specific operation of territoriality with respect to these "Israeli Arabs" will be discussed shortly. As Yiftachel writes,

> The upshot was . . . the penetration of Jews into most Palestinian villages by exclusively Jewish settlements (where non-Jews were not permitted to purchase housing), and the practical ghettoization of the Palestinian minority. In the process, the Palestinian citizens of Israel not only lost individual property, but were also dispossessed of many territorial assets since nearly all state land was earmarked for Jewish use. (1998, 10)

While nearly half of the Palestinian people became refugees, those who remained on the Israeli side of the Green Line became "a trapped minority" (Rabinowitz 2001).

Understood as components of a strategy of (de- and re-) territorializing power, the maneuvers by the state of Israel have also been understood by recent critics as resembling, if not instantiating, "ethnic cleansing" (Falah 1996, 257), "colonial conquest" (Home 2003), and apartheid (Glazer 2003; Halper 2002). Within Israel these initial moves laid the foundations for what Yiftachel calls an "ethnocracy." This is "a specific expression of nationalism that exists in contested territories where a dominant ethnos gains political control and uses the state apparatus to ethnicize the territory and society in question" (2000, 730). What bears emphasis, however one might assess these comparative framings, is the use of violence to enforce claims of control and to effect through territoriality the expulsion, exclusion, and differential inclusion of people, and through these, the shaping of relationships and activities.

The unfolding of territoriality in place in the decades following 1948 is unintelligible without reference to complex processes of identity formation. In play were not only the seemingly self-evident identities of "Jews" and "Arabs," or even "Israelis" and "Palestinians," but the differential formation, achieved in part through territorialization, of "Jewish Israelis" and "Arab Israelis," of "refugees" (now into the third and fourth generation) and non-refugees within the formally non-Israeli sectors of Palestine, of refugees in camps outside of Palestine in other states, and in the wider diasporic spaces farther afield. The constitutive role of territory and identity, in turn, is unintelligible without reference to the complex play of justificatory discourses including, but not limited to, Zionism, expressions of Palestinian nationalism, competing religious discourses and discourses of "democracy," "security," and international humanitarianism, among others.

The effects of the Catastrophe continue to be felt. Indeed, in the decades following 1948 they multiplied. The "right of return" of the refugees and their descendants soon became – and has remained – one of the principal demands of Palestinian activists, but has also remained non-negotiable for most participants.

After 1967

In 1967 an already complex situation (territorially and otherwise) became much more so. Responding to provocative military maneuvers by Egypt, Jordan, and Syria, Israel undertook a preventive attack. Within six days Israel had again defeated these armies and was in control of an enormous amount of additional territory. This included the Sinai Peninsula of Egypt (an area itself much larger than Israel), the Golan Heights of Syria, and, most importantly, the West Bank (including the Arab section of eastern Jerusalem) and the Gaza Strip. That is, all of Palestine – and more – was now under the control of the Israeli military authorities (see map 5). This space was inhabited by more than 1 million Palestinian people. East Jerusalem was annexed immediately, while the remainder of the West Bank and Gaza assumed a new identity as "the Occupied Palestinian Territories." In a later section I will examine how the adjective "occupied" modifies the noun "territories" in practice. For now we might simply note that, along with these occupied territories, another kind of territory appeared. This is the space of "greater Israel" that is contrasted with "Israel proper," or "lesser Israel," that is, the pre-1967 war state west of the Green Line. And it is with respect to the complex interplay between these that the device that Baruch Kimmerling (1989) calls "the Israeli Control System" has operated for nearly 40 years.

"A 'control system'," writes Kimmerling, "is a territorial entity comprising several sub-collectivities, held together by purely military and police forces and their civil extensions (e.g. bureaucracies and settlers)" (1989, 266). Its defining characteristic is "the ruling sector's virtually total lack of interest and ability in creating a common identity or basic value system to legitimize its use of violence to maintain the system, or in

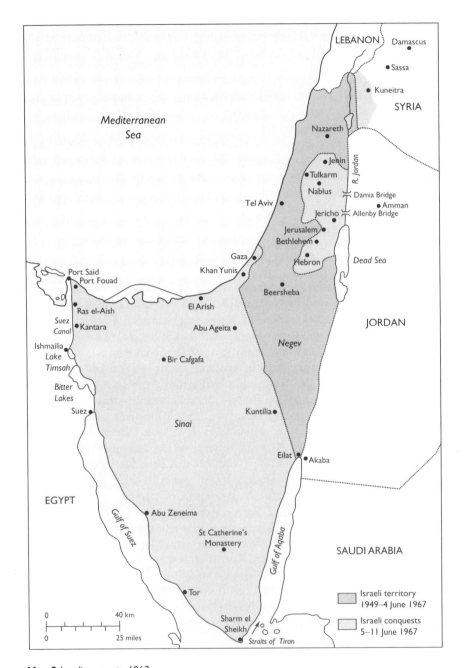

Map 5 *Israeli conquests, 1967*
Source: Bregman 2002. Routledge. Used with permission

developing other kinds of loyalties toward force and power" (p. 266). In contrast to more conventional understandings of territory as marking the clear insides and outsides of social spaces, the precise point of post-1967 territorialization here is to hold the vast majority of Palestinians on the *outside* of "Israel proper" but on the *inside* of the control system of "greater Israel," and to regulate movement between these sectors. Shortly we will examine in greater detail other elements of the Israeli territorial control system in the Occupied Territories. At present I will simply mention a few significant episodes in the territorial unfolding of sovereignty in the nearly 40 years since the occupation was established.

In the period 1977–78 Egypt and Israel began to normalize relations. This resulted, in 1979, in the withdrawal of Israeli forces from Sinai. In 1988 Jordan renounced claims to the West Bank, effectively de-annexing the area. And in 1993 Israel and the Palestinian Liberation Organization formally recognized the legitimacy of each other's existence and began direct negotiations for a settlement of the conflict. One aspect of these negotiations that is particularly relevant to our topic was the agreement on a plan of "phased withdrawal" of Israeli forces and authority from the Occupied Territories and the transfer of some powers to the Palestinian Authority, a governing body headed by Yasser Arafat. According to the plan, which was initially negotiated in talks in Oslo, the Occupied Territories would be divided into non-contiguous zones of three types, called A, B, and C (see map 6). "In Area A, the Palestinians would have full control. In Area B, the Palestinians would control civil society and the two sides would jointly control security. In Area C...Israel would have full control" (Reuveny 2003, 355). The reality, though, is much more complex than this simple mapping would suggest. Even as an aspirational re-territorialization, Area A initially consisted of only 1.1 percent of the West Bank while Area C covered the remainder. As Home explains,

> The effect of the Oslo agreement was to break up the West Bank into some 120 disconnected Palestinian cantons, outside of which development was restricted through planning and other regulations...Even areas ostensibly transferred to the Palestinian Authority were kept under Israeli military control, and there was no physical boundary demarcation between the Palestinian Authority and Israel. (2003, 304)

That is, each micro-enclave of nominal "control" was to be surrounded by Israeli-controlled territory, as would the West Bank as a whole. Some have understood this arrangement as having created an archipelago of dispersed and self-policed open-air prisons. As Edward Said has written, "Israel took 78 percent of Palestine in 1948 and the remaining 22 percent in 1967. Only that 22 percent is in question now" (2001, 33). Israeli

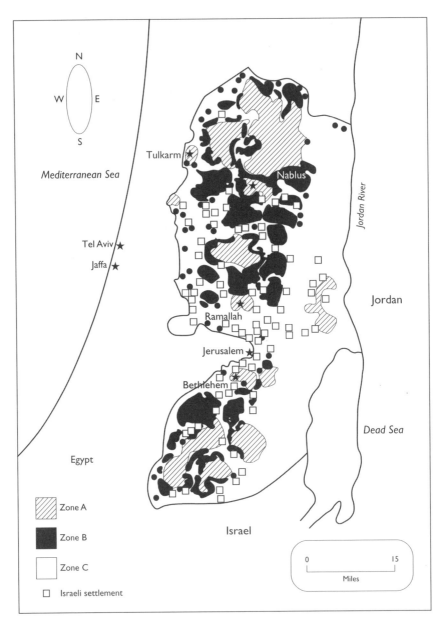

Map 6 *Interim Israeli–Palestinian agreement, 1994*

Source: Bornstein 2002b. University of Pennsylvania Press. Used with permission

anthropologist and anti-occupation activist Jeff Halper likens the Israeli strategy to that of the South African apartheid government and its establishment of "Bantustans" or, essentially, Native reserves that served as containers for unwanted human beings; these were nominally autonomous but were in fact controlled by South Africa. "From Israel's point of view ... the trick is to find an arrangement that would leave it in control of the land, but relieve it of responsibility for the Palestinian population – a kind of occupation by consent" (Halper 2002, 38). A most significant element of this re-territorialization is the accelerated settlement of Jews in the Occupied Territories, a feature that we will examine more closely later in this chapter. The Oslo Agreement was partially implemented, but in the late 1990s began to disintegrate in a horrific spiral of violence. Some militant Palestinian factions rejected not only the agreement but the recognition of Israel's existence, and, indeed, of the PLO's authority to confer that recognition. In response they initiated a series of savage suicide bombings aimed at Israeli civilians within Israel proper, killing hundreds of people. Israel, in turn, responded with massive force. From 1987 to 2004 nearly 4,000 Palestinian civilians were killed and over 26,000 seriously injured (B'Tselem 2003a). At the same time, large segments of the Palestinian people rose up against the occupation in what was called the (second) Intifada or "awakening." This too has been brutally repressed. At the beginning of the twenty-first century the workings of space and violence in Israel/Palestine have resulted in a territoriality of nightmares.

In this section I have been concerned primarily with sketching some of the key episodes through which the territorialization and re-territorialization of sovereignty has unfolded in the area between the Mediterranean Sea and the Jordan River in southwestern Asia. In the 85 years between 1915 and 2000 a given locale, say Nablus, and its inhabitants, began as a somewhat peripheral town in the Ottoman empire, was colonized by Britain under the authority of the League of Nations, was then formally within the nation-state of Jordan, was then occupied by Israel, and, finally, became part of an anomalous, ambiguous collection of non-state entities. Other locales were incorporated into the state of Israel, and their inhabitants either expelled or absorbed. The reconfiguring of territory at this macro-level was accomplished through real-estate transactions, colonial mandates, "Great Power" diplomacy, war, terrorism, and other means. But, in a sense, the territoriality of sovereignty (or effective political-military authority) reveals to us only the most skeletal features of this (or any) territorial regime. At least as significant for everyday life is the territoriality of property or land tenure that conditions other aspects of how lives are lived and of how power circulates through social space.

Reconfiguring Property

As we have already seen, during the pre-Israeli (Ottoman and Mandate) periods Zionism had a well-developed territorial program which aspired to achieve sovereignty through the accumulation and aggregation of units of property. Of course, much of what sovereignty means in practical terms is the unhindered capacity to establish rules within a territory. Within any social order, among the most significant rules are those that pertain to land tenure. In this section I will look at some aspects of the pre-Mandate period law of the land and key transformations of this during the Mandate period. Then I will survey a number of legal mechanisms – that is, formal state directives – by which the state of Israel accomplished the nearly complete Judaization of property during the decades following independence. This is a process that is still unfolding. Its importance for our purposes is in studying the workings of territoriality at a somewhat finer level of analysis than that afforded by an exclusive focus on sovereignty and political colonization.

Prior to the invention of Zionism, Palestinian nationalism, or the arrival of significant numbers of European settlers, the land of Palestine was made legally meaningful by reference to a rather complex system of tenure common throughout much of the Arab world and reflected in Ottoman law. Kimmerling notes that there were "two main patterns of land tenure in Palestine, [and they] had very different degrees of fluidity. The most common form was collective village ownership – *Mushaa*" (1983, 31). "The second major form...was private ownership of large estates" (p. 33). Israeli legal scholar Alexandre Kedar writes that the Ottoman Land Code (OLC),

> defined several categories of land, each with its own specific set of rules. Full ownership of land (entitled *Mulk*) was rare and usually found only at the center of towns and villages. The most common category of land found in populated areas was *Miri*, in which formal and ultimate ownership was held by the State, though a considerable degree of possession and use rights remained in the hands of the individual landholder. Most uninhabited and uncultivated land was defined as *Mewat* (dead) land in which special – and facile – rules over acquisition prevailed. (2001, 932–933)

For our purposes, these categories, referring to specific segments of social space in lived-in landscapes, were integral to and constitutive of the territorial systems of locales. Because each category "had its own specific set of rules," these rules (and their interpretation) structured rights, responsibilities, and relationships with respect to social space. So, for example, "Ottoman law granted the first person to revive dead land (Mewat) the rights to acquire that land ... [O]nly land sufficiently distant from and unused by a local community could qualify as Mewat. According to Article 103 of the OLC ... [e]ven a person who adopted Mewat land for agriculture without official permission had the right to purchase the land" (2001, 934–935). Also, according to Kimmerling, "In addition to the land tenure system there existed (as remnants of the nomadic-tribal society) public rights to land use (*matruka*) whether or not the lands were owned privately, including rights of pasture, irrigation, use of water and passage" (1983, 38). These categories were some of the conceptual resources through which everyday elements of territoriality were made meaningful and practically significant in pre-Zionist Palestine. As Kedar notes, "From a 'modern' perspective, the system of land possession in Palestine during the Ottoman period can be described as unorganized and unclear." But Arab villages

> were usually small communities with a high degree of cohesiveness and familiar long term relationships between community members where unofficial social arrangements for land possession, the terms of which were clearly understood by the participants, developed as alternatives to the official system of registration. (2001, 934)

The OLC of 1858, itself the creation of increasingly centralized authority, "would serve for over a century as one of the cornerstones of the land system of Palestine and then Israel, until the legislation of the Israeli Land Law of 1969" (2001, 932). Thus, the re-territorialization of social life in the region was already under way before the initiation of the Zionist territorial project.

The establishment of large estates, some by way of expropriation by the government and reallocation to absent urban elites living in Beirut or Cairo, had already created a class of absentee landlords and an increasing number of landless laborers (Kimmerling and Migdal 2003). The Zionist project would have proven futile without both willing sellers and some degree of governmental (Ottoman and British) acquiescence. Nonetheless, the purchase of these spaces and the conditions which stipulated that the lands were to remain Jewish constituted a significant transformation in themselves, and were pivotal to the territorial foundation for further dispossession, exclusion, expulsion, and segregation. As I have already noted, these transformations were largely intended and strategic. Kimmerling argues:

> The location of the land purchased was a matter of special concern. The prevailing tendency was to purchase a large tract in a certain area, such as

in the valleys or the coastal plain, and then expand the boundaries of ownership as much as possible. As a result, in several areas a Jewish *territorial continuum* was created which contributed both to the external image of a powerful, homogenous political unit – which went hand in hand with the process of divergence between the Jewish and Arab economies – and to the self-image and sense of security of the Yishuv [the Jewish community]. (1983, 40; emphasis in original)

And there were other effects as well. "When necessary, such territorial continuity made possible effective mutual protection of the settlements, which could quickly come to each other's aid when attacked or threatened, before the national or even local paramilitary organizations acted" (Kimmerling 1983, 40). Furthermore, "as it became clearer, primarily from 1937 onwards, that the physical boundaries of the collectivity would be determined by the 'facts of the field' – that is, the territory of the Jewish state would include all the places owned and settled by Jews – the need was felt to purchase lands, especially in the Galilee and the Negev, which were scattered far from the traditional area of settlement" (p. 40). Kimmerling presents the following quote from a speech presented to the Zionist Executive Committee of 1937:

> We must make an effort to acquire places that are far from the centers of our settlement in order to secure, as much as possible, the boundaries of our country. And indeed when the land purchase programs were established, this goal was always in our minds: to settle the distant areas . . . This is the real conquest of boundaries, from a political standpoint. In this sense, during the last year the JNF decided to expand its activities in order to secure as quickly as possible, the northern and eastern boundaries . . . After all, we are not dealing only with an agricultural matter, for above all we are striving to ensure the broadest possible boundaries for our nation. (quoted in Kimmerling 1983, 40)

These moves were territorial in a number of senses. Most obviously, the particular segments or parcels themselves were territories according to which access, exclusion, and other rights and duties were established and enforced. Because they had been "redeemed" and were held by institutions such as the JNF, they were ethnicized or racialized territories. And by the terms of the strategy they were also conceived of as territorial building blocks of ownership out of which sovereignty could be asserted.

The shift from Ottoman to British colonial authority had important consequences for the re-territorialization of social life generally and for the Judaization (or de-Palestinization) of territory more specifically.

One of the first Mandatory amendments to the OLC was geared to obstruct the facility by which Mewat land could be acquired. The Mewat Land Ordinance (1921) repealed the last paragraph of article 103 [see above] of the OLC, substituting the following in its stead: "Any person who without obtaining the consent of the Administration breaks up or cultivates any waste land shall obtain no right to a title-deed for such land and, further, will be liable to be prosecuted for trespass." The legal implication of this section was potentially immense. Under Ottoman rule, any person who "revived" "dead" or "waste" land immediately acquired good title over it even if he did not receive the authorities' permission. Under the Mandatory rule, such a person became a trespasser no matter how long the person had been cultivating the land. (Kedar 2001, 936)

The British also "modernized" land tenure by instituting a formal registration system.

Zionist organizations exerted pressure on the British government to implement a comprehensive land survey in order to help locate fallow, abandoned State land on which Jews would be able to establish settlements in the spirit of the Balfour Declaration. They also supported the implementation of a process for settling title that would strengthen the reliability of property rights to help facilitate the purchase of privately held land. The combination of Jewish possession and undisputed ownership in land in expanding areas of Palestine was conceived as an important means of Zionist realization of Jewish sovereignty in Palestine. (Kedar 2001, 937–938)

The British

selectively implemented the settlement of titles, focusing on areas that were officially declared "settlement areas" by the authorities. These designations applied mostly to Jewish areas or areas that were subject to dispute between Jews and Arabs but not in the Arab area of Galilee or the Negev. Most of the land that underwent settlement later was included in the territory incorporated into the State of Israel. (Kedar 2001, 939)

The transformations of the land tenure system during the Mandate period (which included a policy in the late 1930s to limit Jewish acquisition), while significant in their own right, pale before those that have taken place since the establishment of Israeli sovereignty. Where only 6 percent of the land in what would become Israel had been owned by Jewish organizations in 1947, by the 1960s they owned more than 94 percent (Kimmerling 1983). Much of this transformation was accomplished by means of laws and the judicial interpretation of these laws (Kedar 2001). Recall that among the most significant consequences of the war of 1948 was the creation, through force and flight, of three-quarters of a million Palestinian refugees (approximately 80 percent of the population) and, for those who fled to locations in areas outside of the state of Israel, the prohibition on their return to their homes, towns, and villages. In *Access Denied: Palestinian Land Rights in Israel* (2003) Hussein and McKay write,

> The main legal instrument that Israel used in order to take possession and control of the land belonging to Palestinian refugees and internally displaced was the Absentees' Property Law 1950. Under the law, all rights in any property belonging to those defined as "absentees" passed automatically to the custodian of Absentee Property. Anyone in possession of absentees' property was bound to hand it over to the Custodian, and failure to do so was made a criminal offence. (p. 70)

The definition of an "absentee" included any Palestinian citizen who had abandoned his place of habitual residence. Technically this definition could apply as much to Jews who were displaced by the war as to Arabs. Indeed, Kedar (2003, 425) quotes one legal commentator as saying, "Did the legislators intend that these regulations would apply also to Israeli Jews resident in Israel[?] If the regulations were meant to apply only to Arabs, then it should be said plainly and clearly." Kedar continues, "Indeed, the regulations included sophisticated mechanisms that resulted in the routine exception of Jews from the status of 'absentees' . . . Simultaneously several tens of thousands of Arabs who became Israeli citizens nevertheless became absentees and acquired the irreconcilable title of 'present absentees' – one that would haunt them for the rest of their lives" (p. 425). This all might reasonably be understood as Sackian "conceptually emptiable space" with a vengeance.

> The Custodian was given sweeping powers to expel people from the land not only unlawful occupiers but also protected tenants where the Custodian decides that the vacation of the land is required "for the purposes of the development of the place or area in which it is situated." . . . [I]n 1953, the Custodian transferred all immovable property under his control to the Development Authority. The Development Authority was in turn authorized by its constitutive legislation to transfer property in its control to the state, to agencies settling Arab internal refugees, or to a local authority, with the stipulation that the JNF be given first option to purchase land . . . During the 1950s and 1960s, Israeli government inspectors were sent out to the Palestinian villages and towns to claim land of those who could be identified as absentees on behalf of the Custodian. Not only villages emptied during the war were affected; the Custodian also asserted his rights

over considerable amounts of land within the Arab communities that survived the war, stepping into the shoes of refugees and asserting their rights over property whether as sole or joint owners of a given piece of land. (Hussein and McKay 2003, 70–73)

A particularly intriguing legal category is that of the "present absentees" or the approximately 75,000 Palestinians who remained in Israel (and became citizens) but who were not at their homes on November 29, 1947. As Peretz has written, "All Arabs who held property in the New City of Acre, regardless of the fact that they may have never traveled farther than the few meters to the Old City, were classified as absentees ... Any individual who may have gone to Beirut or Bethlehem for a one-day visit, during the latter days of the war, was automatically an absentee" (1958, 152, quoted in Kedar 2003, 426). Finally, as Kimmerling notes,

> The Israelification of lands was undertaken by extra-legal means as well. Between 1949 and 1959, Arabs – individuals, villages, and tribes – were compelled to leave their lands. Some were expelled to other areas within Israel and others to places beyond the armistice lines ... the population of the town of Magdal was 9,910 in 1944, while after the war only about 2,500 residents remained. In August 1950 almost all the town's residents were transferred to the Gaza Strip. (1983, 139–140)

The absentee property regulations were not the only formal rules that aimed at (and justified) the radical re-territorialization of life in Israel/Palestine. Other important tools included emergency regulations initially enacted during the Mandate period. Thus, "Under Regulation 125, the Military Governor was empowered to declare 'closed areas' which nobody could enter or leave without a written permit. The areas in which Palestinians lived were divided into small pockets and each was declared a closed area, with movements in and out heavily restricted" (Hussein and McKay 2003, 80). Also, "The Emergency Regulations (Security Zones) 1949 empowered the Minister of Defense to declare areas bordering the frontiers of Israel a security zone and to order any persons to leave such areas. This power was used to expel Palestinians from the villages of Iqrit and Bir'im near the Lebanese border" (2003, 83). The state has also declared areas of Palestinian-owned land to be "Military Areas," or expropriated land under the Public Purpose Ordinance, in which "public" nearly always means Jewish. Another part of the legal machinery of dispossession was the Real Estate Law of 1969, which formally abolished the Ottoman-era land classifications in both Israel proper and the Occupied Territories. "*Matruka* land was registered with the state or local authority, *mawat* [*sic*] with the state, and land outside individual ownership was reclassified as either public real estate or designated real estate (for public benefit), e.g. coastline, road networks" (Home 2003, 297).

The concerted, systematic dispossession, expulsion, exclusion, and destruction of the pre-1948 territorial regime and its thorough "Judaification" has had a number of profound social and existential consequences. Among these, one that is of particular significance for understanding territoriality is the creation of what Israeli sociologist Dan Rabinowitz calls "a trapped minority." This notion aims to elucidate some of the effects that this re-territorialization has had on identity and consciousness among Palestinian Israelis – that is, the descendants of the Arab inhabitants of Israel proper who are citizens of the Israeli state if not members of the Jewish nation. Rabinowitz writes that

> The war which Palestinians lost to Israel in 1948 practically erased their old metropoliti as focuses of belonging and identity. Palestinian centres such as Jaffa, Ramla, Lid, Jerusalem, Bir-Sab'a and their rural hinterlands shrank or disappeared under the rapidly expanding Jewish Israeli strongholds, now inhabited by newly arrived Jewish immigrants from abroad. The Palestinians were largely left with isolated and fragmented villages. The 1950s saw many of those villages lose vast portions of cultivated land and pasture to the Jewish State, mainly through expropriation. (2001, 66)

He continues: "Palestinian citizens of Israel...harbour obvious claims to rights, including rights to land, nevertheless they are consistently excluded from most political processes that determine land use, development and well-being in their very homeland" (p. 66). Moreover, "The spatial discontinuity that has ensued damaged the Palestinians' sense of communal time, and their ability to forge a coherent identity" (pp. 66–67). Rabinowitz is suggesting that the re-territorialization of social space has brought about a sort of partitioning of collective consciousness and identity. But the principal effect of this is the creation of a sense of "suffocation" (p. 67). "Palestinians in northern Israel can locate and relocate only within a small triangle that includes parts of Acre, Nazareth and Haifa. The rest of the country, while formally accessible to all, is effectively out of bounds for them" (p. 67).

Rabinowitz brings out some of the experiential dimensions of this territorial process: "Entrapment is a dramatic development. A space initially perceived to be safe is subject to sudden external interference leading to confinement: a door is closed, a fence erected, a wall cemented. The space becomes a dangerous enclosure. The subject is suddenly incarcerated" (p. 73). This incarceration, in turn, engenders other effects. Rabinowitz argues that trapped minorities suffer a double marginalization. First, they are marginalized within the state. "The dominant group that hegemonizes the new state that entraps the minority tends to treat its members as less than equal citizens" (p. 73). But at the same time, "seen from the Arab world,"

> The Palestinian citizens of Israel emerge as an ambiguous and problematic element whose status in the national arena is yet to be determined, and whose very loyalty to the Palestinian nation is suspect... In the 1960s and 1970s, for example, the Palestinian citizens of Israel were treated by the exiled Palestinian leadership as a self-seeking, spoilt collective, collaborating with the Zionist occupation of their homeland... A trapped minority is likely to remain non-assimilating... Torn between the culture of its mother nation and its host state, members of a trapped minority have difficulty in participating in the production and consumption of language, theatre, music, cinema, media and folklore in the hegemonic culture of the state particularly where such production involves exclusive signification of national identity. (Rabinowitz 2001, 74, 76–77)

Relatedly, "members of trapped minorities are likely to display chronic ideological and political internal divisions, and to experience difficulties in forging a united front both inside and outside the state" (p. 77). That is, territorial reconfigurations are here understood as inducing ideological divisions and divergences. But, of course, it isn't simply that Palestinian Israelis and Palestinians outside of "Israel proper" (especially those in the Occupied Territories) are on different sides of a border (and here it is important to recognize that families may be divided and that members of territorially divided families may live within a few miles of each other); it is that they occupy different locations within constellations of power that are themselves strongly, if incompletely, territorialized. And the entrapment is not only spatial. It also has temporal aspects that intersect with territoriality. From the perspective of the dominant Zionist discourse, "The Arab minority... was treated as if it surfaced out of nowhere. Its history was truncated, its spatial continuity with Palestinians and Arabs in adjacent territories arrested. Its entrapment as a figment of the Israeli presence was complete" (Rabinowitz 2001, 80). But on the other hand, from within that same discourse the differences that territory might make – that is, the possible differences between Palestinian citizens of the state and the larger number of Palestinian enemies of the state beyond the Green Line – can be easily effaced. "A trapped minority is, by definition, not easily contained: it spreads across the borders into other territories, adjacent or abroad, forging pacts with enemies and strangers... The metaphor of aliens as agents of disease – a foreign entity that invades the body nation, threatening to destroy it from within – often surfaces in rhetoric that reflects the majority's darkest xenophobic fear and hatred. Being a trapped minority thus emerges as not merely complicated and confusing, but also as potentially dangerous" (pp. 78–79).

The Israeli Territorial System of Control

If Palestinian citizens of Israel are a trapped minority the Palestinians who live in the Occupied Territories are a trapped majority. And they are multiply trapped at that. In this section I will sketch primary elements of the Israeli territorial control system in the Occupied Territories at a finer level of detail than that afforded by analysis of property and sovereignty. Ultimately what is implicated here are the Goffman-like "territories of the self" discussed in chapter 2.

The place to begin is the simple fact of occupation itself. Recall that the West Bank and Gaza Strip were not annexed by Israel (with the exception of east Jerusalem and the Golan Heights). They are "occupied," that is, controlled by the military and by other agents of the state while remaining formally other than and outside of that state. As we will discuss in more detail below, the territories are also increasingly occupied by Israeli civilians in fortified "settlements." Occupation is, of course, a kind of territorial relationship. Territory is the space within which occupation takes place. But it is not just the territories that are occupied. People, lives, time – social reality – are all occupied, that is, controlled by and for the benefit of others. Nothing is untouched by the processes and practices of occupation. Occupation means nothing without the routine deployment of violence and humiliation for the purposes of maintaining power. The occupation is made meaningful to the occupiers and to relevant observers through a discourse of "security" in combination with the Zionist discourse of the redemption of Samaria and Judea. The Occupied Territories are non-state, non-sovereign spaces. Formally, the 3.6 million people who live in these spaces are not citizens and they have no state to protect them from the violence of others. Formally, of course, they have human rights, but these too are routinely violated (Amnesty International 2003). Functionally, then, the Occupied Territories are colonies of Israel. In this section I will simply catalogue some of the principal components of the territorial system: the Green Line, the camps, the checkpoints, closures and curfews, the settlements, the geopolitics of verticality, and the barrier wall and seam area.

The Green Line

The Occupied Territories are in two disconnected pieces (see map 4). The West Bank is landlocked and, in any case, Israel controls the borders with

Israel proper and with Jordan. As noted above, the whole of the West Bank can be understood as analogous to a large Native reserve. As we saw, analogies have also been made with apartheid-era Bantustans and to open-air prisons. Israel controls ingress, egress, and air space. Gaza is a tiny, very densely populated strip of land on the coast. Its border with Egypt is closed. Economically, however, the Occupied Territories are tightly integrated with Israel. There is little work and, especially since the 1990s, the unemployment rates are very high. From 1967 to the 1990s the border between Israel proper and the territories was relatively open and Palestinians were an important source of relatively cheap labor for Israeli businesses. Since the Intifada the border has been periodically closed. This, of course, has a profound effect on Palestinian economic conditions. More recently Israel has imported replacement workers from places as far away as Bolivia and Ghana (Bartram 1996).

Avram Bornstein, an American anthropologist who has lived in the West Bank and written an ethnography of the Green Line, writes:

> For those in the West Bank, the Green line (the former Jordanian Israeli armistice line that separates the West Bank from Israel proper) shaped everyday life, more than ever, in the opportunities to make a living. Border policies restricted Palestinian agriculture and industry, pushing many to serve Israeli producers and consumers. Tens of thousands of West Bank workers crossed the border to work in Israel almost every day. Tens of thousands of others, like car mechanics and textile workers, worked for Israelis in the West Bank. The border limited the claims most of these workers could make on those who made the profits. Subcontracting agents, who made business across the border possible, also suffered restrictions at the border, but the border brought them new sources of wealth, creating new internal tensions. Labor and production processes in the borderland were an important part of the national conflict often missed in descriptions of the Israel–Palestinian struggle. (2002b, ix)

The Green Line, then, not only separates, it integrates. It does so, how-ever, under conditions of extreme inequality. This facilitates what Born-stein has elsewhere called "superexploitation" (2002a). But while it may integrate in some ways, in other ways it promotes the divergence of Palestinian identities.

> The border became a location separating cultural worlds. The customs of gender, age, and marriage of most West Bankers were demonstrably dif-ferent from those of their relatives only a few kilometers away across the border. Palestinians were marking inter-ethnic and intra-ethnic cultural borders. Customs indicated inequalities and solidarities, and reinscribed relations made by the border as well as the personal identities they imply.

The making of borders established a distinction and connection between West Bank and Israeli Palestinians and also distinguished those who remained inside historic Palestine and those in diaspora communities in Jordan, the Gulf, and beyond. (2002b, xi)

The effects of territoriality are also facilitated through the deployment of what Bornstein calls a "color-coded bureaucracy":

West Bank residents carried their identification card in orange-colored holders, Gazans had red and Israelis had blue. Similarly, cars were easily distinguishable by their color-coded license plates: Israelis had yellow, West Bankers had blue. The West Bank blue plates also had a Hebrew letter that identified the district in which the car was registered. (2002b, 206)

The border, as we shall see, is opened and closed at will by the Israeli authorities, sometimes in ways that appear to be quite arbitrary:

Even when the checkpoint was open, it was a place where heavily armed soldiers were looking for reasons to open fire or take people into custody. This alone made crossings dangerous. Passing through it could be the first step into detention, which could unfold into an experience of incarceration and torture while under interrogation. This potential threat of physical violence also made symbolic violence all too common. Palestinians often faced the simple but painful humiliation of a soldier's disrespectful questioning or search. Even if none of these things happened, crossing the Green Line peacefully was a form of economic violence that limited the rights of workers and the potential of Palestinian businesses... The geopolitical border is an important form of acute violence that often underlies structural forms of violence. (2002b, 16)

This is territoriality at work in the lives of both the controlled and the controllers.

The border separating the Gaza Strip from Israel is an electrified fence. In order to enter Israel from Gaza Palestinians are required to pass through five screening stations. According to Israeli journalist and anti-occupation activist Amira Hass, "The fifth screening station is a row of nineteen turnstiles that open onto what is called "Israel square," the Israeli zone. Here the computer monitors, metal detectors, and electronic gates enforce efficient and relentless security – anyone who has slipped through this far will go no further" (1999, 268). Israeli settlers face no obstacles crossing into Gaza. Reflecting a kind of inverted territorial consciousness, Hass writes, "The word *inside* has... been upended. The land within Israel's 1967 borders, including all the Palestinian cities and villages, is referred to as 'inside,' partly as a way to avoid saying Israel's name but also because of the geopolitical fact that up until 1967 all the refugees from inside the borders lived outside of them ... In a 147 square mile ribbon of land with no exit, 'inside' has become synonymous with wide open spaces" (1999, 170).

The camps

A key component of the Israeli territorial control system are the so-called refugee camps where the expelled and their descendants landed. They are "so-called" because, while most of the residents of these spaces retain the legal status "refugee," the vast majority were born to this territorially defined status and have never been to their homeland. Also, if the word "camp" suggests temporary shelter, Palestinian refugee camps, some now more than 50 years old, are more like squalid urban neighborhoods. If some Palestinians on the other side of the Green Line are "Present Absentees," many on the outside are "Permanent Temporaries." One-third of Palestinian people are registered as refugees; one-third of these refugees live in camps in Syria, Jordan, and Lebanon; 40 percent of the people in the West Bank and 70 percent of Gazans are refugees (www.un.org/unrwa). The camps constitute a geography of dispersal and containment. Some services are provided by the United Nations Relief and Works Agency for Palestine. This is the largest United Nations agency. It is also the largest employer of Palestinians.

> There are eight camps in the Gaza Strip, and some 339,000 human beings, 55% of the refugees, make their homes in them. The rest of the refugees, about 320,000 people, have been scattered throughout Gaza's old and new residential neighborhoods. In al-Shatti camp on the outskirts of Gaza City, 186 acres house 66,000 human beings. Al-Boureji, in the center of the Strip, used to be a British army camp. In 1948, some 13,000 refugees who gathered there were housed in old army huts, while the rest lived in tents near the camp, on a total of 132 acres. Today that number has swelled to 27,000. (Hass 1999, 171)

Just as the Green Line partitions the identity and consciousness of Palestinians, so the camps further partition the identities and conscious-nesses of Palestinians in the Occupied Territories. There are pronounced perceived differences between camp residents, and non-refugee Gazan natives, or *muwataneen*. As one of Hass's informants reports,

> Whenever I went to the market with my mother, she'd point out the border between the camp and the city ... We'd [the *mehajers*] go out to demonstrate

against the soldiers but the *muwataneen* kids wouldn't join us. And when we ran into the orange groves to get away from the soldiers, the *muwataneen* chased us away because they were afraid. I began to think that the city kids were on good terms with the occupation. (Hass 1999, 176)

Likewise in the West Bank, Bornstein reports that

boys from the camp were watched with suspicion when in the village. They were generally not greeted, as other villagers were, with polite calls of welcome. There were some friendships, but they seemed rare...The high-school students from the village had to walk an extra kilometer to get to school in the main town because they walked around the camp rather than through it. (2002b, 20)

The territorialization of consciousness is also apparent among diasporic Palestinians. Writing specifically about refugees in other Arab countries, Peretz claims that "A major difference in outlook between Palestinians in the camps and those outside is the extent to which camp residents are submerged in Palestinian consciousness...Even though the children, and in many cases their parents have never seen Palestine. they believe that Palestine is their homeland" (1993, 27). As territories of containment the camps can be closed off at will by the Israeli authorities and the military routinely enter the camps in search of militants.

The checkpoints

Whether or not in formal camps, a pervasive territorial system of control operates throughout the Occupied Territories. The Oslo Agreement, as we noted, produced "a confusing mosaic of pieces of territory with differing status ('A,' 'B,' and 'C') depending on the nature of the security control over them... most of the population living in scattered islands of A and B, separated from each other by vast oceans of C lands, hundreds of villages and half a dozen towns could be totally paralyzed by strategically placed barricades and ditches, tanks and [Israeli Army] sharpshooters, thereby devastating an entire economy and disrupting all social life" (Hass 2002, 9). Throughout the West Bank and Gaza an immense "matrix of control" (Halper 2000) has been put into place, consisting of checkpoints, permits, passes, closures, and curfews that effectively immobilize all of the Palestinian people for days or even weeks.

Amnesty International reports that in August 2003 there were over 300 Israeli checkpoints and roadblocks in the Occupied Territories.

At checkpoints, soldiers often check cars or pedestrians slowly, sometimes stopping the flow of traffic and refusing to examine an identity card without explanation. On occasion, crowds build up at checkpoints and soldiers fire into the air or throw sound bombs or tear gas to disperse them. Internal closures frequently operate in an arbitrary way. The fact that soldiers enjoy broad, individual discretion to permit or prevent Palestinians' movement undermines the Israeli authorities' contention that the internal closure is a rational system, based on strict security needs. (Amnesty International 2003, 19)

The experiential effects for those on the receiving end of these territorial operations are also detailed in the Amnesty International report. "Ordinary activities, such as going to work or to school, taking a baby for immunization, attending a funeral or a wedding, expose women and men, young and old, to such risks. Hence, many people limit their activities outside the home to what is absolutely essential" (2003, 4).

The micro-territoriality of power is expressed through a complex system of permits and passes. This was already mentioned in connection with the Green Line, but it is much more pervasive.

The pass system turned a universal basic right into a coveted privilege – or portion of a privilege – allotted to a minority on a case by case basis. For the privilege was not whole: it had gradations. Some passes permitted an overnight stay in Israel, others required return by dusk, a few were for an entire month...The hand that giveth also taketh away: some months as many as 1,000 businessmen might be granted passes, other months only 300; sometimes the passes for Gazans would be for Israel and the West Bank, sometimes only for the West Bank. It was thus that an entire society was stratified and segmented on the basis of whether one had access, and in what portion, to the "privilege" of freedom of movement. (Hass 2002, 8)

A human rights attorney testified to Amnesty International about the experience of the permit and pass system: "Every time I drive on these roads and see a tank in the distance I wonder if I'll make it home to see my children again. I have a permit, for a month, but if the soldiers shoot at me and I am killed the permit won't do any good to me or to my family" (Amnesty International 2003, 17).

Hass characterizes this hyper-territorialization as effecting "the theft of time" as Palestinian people "found that they could no longer make any plans: it was impossible to know until the very last minute whether one could get the necessary permit. While not being able to plan ahead, they also lost the ability to act spontaneously – and spontaneity is no less a human right than travel or food" (2002, 10). She suggests that these experiential dimensions of the system are an intended consequence. She speaks of "the need to plead, to beg, the prospect of being turned down, the anger, the repeated trips to the liaison office . . . the visit to an Israeli officer who suggests, 'If you help us, we'll help you' – meaning, 'Become a collaborator, and you'll get your permit.'" (p. 11).

Closures and curfews

Another aspect of the territorial system is the policy of "closures." "Internal" closures refer to the virtual lock-down of the Occupied Territories. Under closure all permits are suspended. Amnesty International reports that

> The first comprehensive internal closure, in March 1996, lasted for 21 days. In 1997 a total of 27 days of internal closure were imposed on all or part of the West Bank; in 1998, the total was 40 days. The internal closures demonstrate how Israel . . . could bring Palestinian life to a halt and the Palestinian economy to its knees through its control of the areas and main roads around the supposedly autonomous Palestinian enclaves. (2003, 14)

Hass says that "Closure is no longer the abstract, bureaucratic procedure of asking for a permit and being rejected. Closure has become part of Palestinian human and natural topography" (2002, 12). Closure also has the effect of fragmenting the West Bank and Gaza and disconnecting one from the other. As one Palestinian has said, "We're like birds in a cage" (quoted in Smith 2001).

A related device for territorializing everyday life is the imposition of curfews which constrict the space of movement to the confines of one's home. Again, from the Amnesty International report: "Some villages have been completely sealed off and urban areas are frequently placed under 24-hour curfew, during which no one is allowed to leave the house, often for prolonged periods" (2003, 3). They report that, during March and April of 2002, "Bethlehem was under curfew for 40 consecutive days" (p. 20) and that "on 9 July 2002 almost half the population of the West Bank, nearly 900,000 out of some 2.2 million Palestinians, were under curfew in 71 different localities" (p. 21). Penalties for breaking curfew – that is, for leaving one's home – are severe and include the very real possibility of being killed. Some entire villages, such as al-Mawasi in Gaza, "have been declared closed military areas . . . Residents are allowed to enter and leave the areas only on foot and only between certain specified times, but at times the army stops all residents from leaving or returning to the areas for days at a time . . . and a dusk to dawn curfew is usually in force" (p. 23)

The settlements and bypass roads

Yet another profoundly important element in the territorial control system in the Occupied Territories is the constellation of exclusive Jewish "settlements" that have been established in the West Bank and Gaza (as well as in the Golan Heights) since 1967. David Newman asserts that "Settlements have played, and continue to play, a major role in the delimitation of boundaries between separate Israeli and Palestinian territories, regardless of whether they were established legally" (2002, 635). Over half of the West Bank is owned by Israel. Israeli policy, especially since 1977 and accelerating during the 1990s, has involved the civilian colonization of the Occupied Territories through the building of enclaves for Israeli "settlers." In 1977, 5,000 Israelis lived in settlements in the West Bank; by 2001 more than 200,000 Israelis lived in 137 settlements in the West Bank and seven settlements in the Gaza Strip. Many of these were set up by religious fundamentalists driven by an ideology of the "redemption" of Judea and Samaria (biblical names for the West Bank) (Newman 1985). Some are effectively bedroom commuter villas for Israelis who work in Jerusalem or Tel Aviv. Some, like Ma'ale Edummim, are instant cities in their own right.

As in the pre-Mandate and Mandate eras the objective is to establish "facts on the ground." As the designer of Ma'ale Edummim, Thomas Leitersdorf, has said, "The strategy in Judea and Samaria at the time was to "capture ground": you capture as much area as possible by placing a few people on numerous hills. The underlying political idea was that the further inside the Occupied Territories we place settlers, the more territory Israel would have when the time came to set the permanent international borders – because we were already there" (Tamir-Tawil 2003, 152). Indeed, the system of closures, curfews, and permits is often explicitly justified as existing for the benefit of the settlers. Thus in Gaza literally hundreds of thousands of Palestinians are routinely immobilized for the convenience of a few thousand settlers. David Newman writes,

> While Israelis are reticent to use the term, establishing civilian settlements in this way is part of the process of landscape colonization through which territories are brought under long term control by the dominant power and/ or those aspiring to future statehood and hegemony. It is accomplished by implanting civilian populations expected to sink roots and develop a sense of bonding with the territory in question. Future generations born within these communities would perceive this to be their "natural homeland." (2002, 636)

Settlements play multiple roles in a complex territorial strategy. In the first place they are extra-territorial spores of Israel proper dispersed throughout the Occupied Territories. For example, as the Israeli human rights organization B'Tselem states in its report *Land Grab: Israeli Settlement Policy in the West Bank*,

> any Israeli citizen, and indeed any Jew...in the Occupied Territories is subject, wherever they may be, to the authority of Israeli civilian law for almost all purposes, and not to the authority of the military law applying to these territories...Settlers elect their local or regional council, participate in Knesset elections, pay taxes, National Insurance, health insurance, and enjoy all the social rights granted by Israel to its citizens. (2002, 52)

That is to say, Israelis are not considered to have crossed a meaningful border while in the Occupied Territories. They are still, effectively, "inside." In a sense, the Green Line always surrounds them. Needless to say, Palestinians are prohibited from entering the settlement enclaves except as laborers. B'Tselem reports that even sparsely populated settlements may encompass vast areas of the Occupied Territories:

> The areas of jurisdiction of the regional councils in the West Bank include enormous empty areas (approximately thirty-five percent of the area of the West Bank) that are not attached to the area of any specific settlement. These areas constitute the reserves of land for future expansion of the settlements, or for the establishment of industrial zones...Various areas within the regional councils' areas of jurisdiction in the West Bank are defined as "firing zones" and are used by the IDF for military exercises. Other areas are now defined as "nature reserves," where any form of development is prohibited. (2002, 70)

Settlement space may virtually surround Palestinian towns such that expansion may be effectively prohibited. This strongly exacerbates overcrowding. B'Tselem, for example, reports that "The urban area of the city of Nablus, which includes eight villages and two refugee camps that are completely contiguous with the city...is surrounded on almost all sides by settlements blocking the city's development" (2002, 95). The borders of individual settlements may be drawn in such a way as to form a contiguous "bloc" (p. 96). Also, Palestinian land may be "trapped" inside of settlements. "Construction on these islands is not allowed – they still legally belong to the Palestinian owner, who, however, most often has no access to it" (Weizman 2002).

The geopolitics of verticality

Among the most thorough examinations of the territorial functions and effects of the settlements is that undertaken by Israeli architect Eyal Weizman and his colleagues, most notably in *The Politics of Verticality* (2002) and *A Civilian Occupation: The Politics of Israeli Architecture* (Segal and Weizman 2003). Weizman describes the territorial function of settlements this way: "Not only places of residence, they [the Jewish settlements] create a large-scale network of 'civilian fortification' which is part of the army's regional plan of defence, generating tactical territorial surveillance. A simple act of domesticity, a single family home shrouded in the cosmetic façade of red tiles and green lawns, conforms to the aims of territorial control" (2002). The project of territorial control is reflected in the physical layout of the settlements:

> the form of the mountain settlements is constructed according to a geometric system that unites the effectiveness of sight with spatial order, producing "panoptic fortresses", generating gazes to many different ends. Control – in the overlooking of Arab town and villages; strategy – in the overlooking of main traffic arteries; self-defence – in the overlooking of the immediate surroundings and approach roads. Settlements could be seen as urban optical devices for surveillance and the exercise of power. (2002)

And, at a finer level of analysis, the territorial project conditions the internal geometry of the settlements. "The 'panopticon fortress' principle applies most easily to the outer ring of homes. The inner rings are positioned in front of the gaps between the homes of the first ring. This arrangement of the homes around summits, outward-looking, imposes on the dwellers axial visibility (and lateral invisibility), oriented in two directions: inward and outward" (2002). Indeed, the project even finds expression in the interior design of the houses. Weizman writes that architectural guidelines on design recommend

> the orientation of the sleeping rooms towards the inner public spaces and the living rooms towards the distant view. The inward-oriented gaze protects the soft cores of the settlements, the outward-oriented one surveys the landscape below. Vision dictated the discipline and mode of design on every level, even down to the precise positioning of windows ... (2002)

And, finally, the bodies of the settlers themselves are incorporated into the Israeli Territorial System of control. "Knowingly or not, settlers' eyes, seeking a completely different view, are being 'hijacked' for strategic and geopolitical aims" of the Israeli state (2002). This astonishingly detailed and complex territorial configuration goes well beyond the model of classification, communication, and enforcement. The settlement complex constitutes what Weizman has called a "politics of verticality."

An important integrating element of the territorial control system is the network of "bypass roads." These are limited access roads (which Palestinians are prohibited from using) that connect the settlements with Israel proper and with each other. They run for a total length of more than 340 kilometers and have entailed the confiscation of thousands of acres of land in the Occupied Territories. This has resulted in the destruction of hundreds of Palestinian homes and of olive groves and other productive agricultural land (Meehan 1996). Weizman reads the emerging political topography this way:

> The bypass roads attempt to separate Israeli traffic networks from Palestinian ones, preferably without allowing them ever to cross. They emphasize the overlapping of two separate geographies that inhabit the same landscape. At points where the networks do cross, a makeshift separation is created. Most often, small dust roads are dug out to allow Palestinians to cross under the fast, wide highways on which Israeli vans and military vehicles rush between settlements...Meron Benvenisti writes: "And indeed the person traveling on the longest bridge in the country and penetrating the earth in the longest tunnel may ignore the fact that over his head there is a whole Palestinian town and that on his way he does not come across any Arab, save for some drivers that dare go on the Jewish road."
> (2002)

Indeed, Benvenisti, a former deputy mayor of Jerusalem, has described the emerging territorial configuration as a process of crashing "three-dimensional space into six dimensions – three Jewish and three Arab." The geopolitics of verticality extends to airspace and to sub-surface space. Israel holds control of the airspace over the West Bank. It uses its domination of the airspace and electromagnetic spectrum to drop a net of surveillance and pinpoint executions over the territory.

> Complete control over the West Bank's airspace is currently exercised by the Israeli Defence Force (IDF). In Camp David, Israel agreed to the concept of a Palestinian state, but demanded sovereignty over the airspace above it in the context of a final resolution...During the Oslo and Camp David negotiations, Israel insisted on keeping control of the underground resources in any permanent resolution. A new form of subterranean sovereignty, which erodes the basics of national sovereignty, is first mentioned in the Oslo Interim Accord. (Weizman 2002)

The seam area and the wall

The most recent addition to the Israeli territorial control system is the "separation barrier" or, more starkly, "the wall" (B'Tselem 2003b; Cook 2003; Levy 2003; Perry 2003). This is a 25-foot-high, concrete, steel and barbed wire structure that was begun in 2002 and, when completed, will wind its way more than 600 kilometers through the West Bank (see the cover illustration). In form it is said to resemble "a string of Norwegian fjords" (Rappaport 2003) due the twists, turns, and loops that reflect the countless decisions about what and who will be placed east and west of the structure. The stated purpose of the wall is to prevent the entry of terrorists into Israel proper. But the wall does not follow the Green Line. In some places it cuts deeply into the Occupied Territories. When it is finished tens of thousands of Palestinians and a number of whole villages will be east of the Green Line but west of the wall in an ultra-anomalous territory called "the seam area" (B'Tselem 2003b). For example, the wall will separate the villagers of Baka Sharkiya and Bartaa Sharkiya

> from their Palestinian brothers in the West Bank and in order to go to Jenin to buy something or sell something, they will have to pass a border crossing, which is unclear when and where it will be. It is also not clear how they will receive basic services such as schools or health services from the [Palestinian Authority], which will be on the other side of the fence. While there will be no fence between them and Israel, in Israel they will be considered illegal residents, and there is no intention to annex them or turn them into Israeli citizens. (Rappaport 2003)

Not incidentally, almost 40 percent of the West Bank's agricultural area and two-thirds of its water resources will be on the Israel side of the wall. Some villages will be split by the wall, and the houses of many farmers will be on one side and their fields and groves on the other. Some houses will be almost entirely surrounded by the wall (Archer 2004). The wall will have locked gates that can be opened only by Israeli military personnel. B'Tselem reports that

> All Palestinians over the age of twelve who live in the seam area will be required to obtain a "permanent resident permit" from the Civil Administration to enable them to continue to live in their homes. Palestinian residents whose request for a permit is rejected may argue their case before a military committee. If the committee denies the appeal, they must leave their homes...Palestinians with farmland in the seam area will have to provide "documents indicating the applicants' right to the land"; teachers in the villages in the seam area will have to present certificates proving they are authorized teachers. The permits must indicate a certain gate through

which the holder of the permit must cross, and the times of day at which the holder is allowed to pass. Sleeping over in the seam area, bringing a vehicle into the area, and transporting merchandise into the area require separate permits. (B'Tselem 2003b)

As Meron Rappaport has written, "The only thing left the Palestinians is to live in huge pens and to work in the industrial zones that will no doubt be built in the settlements, near the openings to these pens" (2003).

Concluding Remarks

This chapter has traced the unfolding of some of the principal components of one of the most intensively territorialized control systems ever created. Its objective was to provide a detailed illustration of many of the themes discussed in the previous chapters. In the making, remaking, and operation of the Israeli territorial control system can be seen the constitutive role of various ideologies and discourses (sovereignty, nationalisms, property, colonialism, religious fundamentalisms, human rights); the interplay between territorial structures and various trajectories of mobility (immigration, eviction, expulsion, invasion, occupation); a range of disparate practices (land purchases, diplomacy, warfare, legal interpretation, extra-legal violence); and the fluid articulation and disarticulation of "vertical" scales of analysis and experience (corporeal, local, national, regional, international). In rendering this sketch I have drawn on observations of scholars from a number of disciplines and of activists. We would do well to recall the words of David Newman with which this chapter began. Examining the territorial parsing of "Palisraelestine" "shows how important the territorial dimension remains for understanding the political organization of space, even in this 'borderless and deterritorialized' world and smallest of territories" (2002, 632).

This rendering is admittedly "one-sided" insofar as its focus is on the construction and operation of the Israeli territorial control system and its effects on the Palestinian people. This is chiefly the result of the radical asymmetries of power involved here. While the Palestinian people are by no means absolutely powerless in shaping the spaces within which they and the Israeli people live and die, clearly their capacity to do so is significantly less than that of the Israeli state. The one-sidedness of my rendering is somewhat mitigated, though, by my heavy reliance on the interpretation of Israeli scholars and activists who are critical of the territorial control system within which their lives and the lives of their loved ones are enclosed. To some extent the struggle between Palestinians and Israelis is mirrored (albeit not fully) in debates between Zionist and anti-Zionist, religious and secular, conservative, liberal, and radical, young and old Israelis who will continue to re-territorialize the conditions of human existence in the land adjacent to the southeastern corner of the Mediterranean Sea. The territorial configurations now in place reflect the forces of fear, hatred, cruelty, corruption, betrayal, and sacrifice. Against all odds many aspire to create configurations conducive to the furtherance of hope, respect, and human dignity.

5

Further Explorations

The preceding chapters sought to demonstrate both that territory and territoriality are more complex than is commonly acknowledged and that there are, nevertheless, a number of features that allow us to make sense of them across a wide range of contexts. An interdisciplinary approach is useful for seeing territory and for seeing through and around territory from different angles. While each of the disciplines provide useful interpretive resources, too cloistered a view has the tendency to obscure – to limit, to put out of bounds – the insights of the other disciplines. Territory, as we have seen, is expressed not only at international borders and not only on front lawns. We – each and all – navigate innumerable territories, encounter countless territorializations, participate in the marking or evasion of innumerable boundaries and borders simply by living our lives. Because territories are expressions of the fusion of power, meaning, and social space, and because these connections are often contingent, contested, or unstable, we – each and all – participate in the never-ending processes of making and remaking our worlds. As I have stressed throughout this book, where territory matters most is in the conditioning of human experience. But while all of our lives shape and are shaped by territorial configurations, each of us is differently situated with respect to the myriad insides and outsides that territoriality inscribes on our worlds.

The interdisciplinary approach that I have sketched is not without drawbacks in a Short Introduction. Most obviously, in order to "make space" for a wider range of disciplinary perspectives, any given perspective will necessarily be treated less thoroughly. As was suggested in chapter 2, the present era can justly be regarded as something of a golden age for the debate and retheorization of territoriality. More scholars from a wider range of disciplines are bringing an increasingly diverse set of theoretical resources and empirical case studies to bear on the topic than ever before. As was also suggested, this may itself be due to the fact that territorial configurations that condition our lives are so clearly in flux. The objective of this brief chapter is to draw attention to some resources that were not discussed in previous chapters. In political geography the books by Cox and Storey are particularly good complements to the present volume.

Books

Anthropology

Cieraad I ed. 1999 *At Home: An Anthropology of Space* Syracuse University Press, Syracuse.
Coakley P ed. 2003 *The Territorial Management of Ethnic Conflict* Frank Cass, London.
Das V and Poole D eds. 2004 *Anthropology in the Margins of the State* School of American Research Advanced Seminar Series, Santa Fe.
Donnan H and Wilson T eds. 1994 *Border Approaches* University Press of America, Lanham, MD.
Pellow D ed. 1996 *Setting Boundaries: The Anthropology of Spatial and Social Organization* Bergin & Garvey, Westport, CT.

Architecture

Deutsch R 1996 *Evictions: Art and Spatial Politics* MIT Press, Cambridge, MA.
Pearson M and Richards C 1997 *Architecture and Order: Approaches to Social Space* Routledge, London.
Unwin S 2000 *An Architecture Notebook: Wall* Routledge, London.

Boundaries

Berg E and Van Houtum H 2003 *Routing Borders Between Territories: Discourses and Practices* Ashgate, Burlington, VT.
Buchanan A and Moore M eds. 2003 *States, Nations and Borders: The Ethics of Making Boundaries* Cambridge University Press, Cambridge.
Miller D and Hashmi S eds. 2001 *Boundaries and Ethics: Diverse Ethical Perspectives* Princeton University Press, Princeton, NJ.

Critical geopolitics

Herod A, Ó Tuathail G and Roberts S eds. 1998 *Unruly World: Globalization, Governance and Geography* Routledge, London.

Newman D ed. 1999 *Boundaries, Territory and Post-modernity* Frank Cass, London.
Ó Tuathail G and Dalby S eds. 1998 *Rethinking Geopolitics* Routledge, London.
Ó Tuathail G, Dalby S and Routledge P eds. 1998 *The Geopolitics Reader*. Routledge, London.

Environmental psychology

Altman I 1975 *The Environment and Social Behavior: Privacy, Personal Space, Territory and Crowding* Brooks-Cole, Monterey, CA.
Kirby K 1996 *Indifferent Boundaries: Spatial Concepts of Human Subjectivity* Guilford, New York.

Geopolitics

Agnew J 2003 *Geopolitics: Re-Visioning World Politics* Routledge, London.
Cohen S 2003 *Geopolitics of the World System* Rowman & Littlefield, Lanham, MD.
Derlugian G and Greer S eds. 2000 *Questioning Geopolitics: Political Prospects in a Changing World System* Greenwood Press, Westport, CT.
Kliot D and Newman D eds. 2000 *Geopolitics at the End of the 20th Century: The Changing World Map* Frank Cass, London.
Sempra F 2002 *Geopolitics from the Cold War to the 21st Century* Transactions, New Brunswick, NJ.

International relations

Anderson M 1996 *Frontiers, Territory and State Formation in the Modern World* Polity Press, Cambridge.
Huth P 1996 *Standing Your Ground: Territorial Disputes and International Conflict* University of Michigan Press, Ann Arbor.
Kacowicz A 1994 *Peaceful Territorial Change* University of South Carolina Press, Columbia.
O'Leary B, Lustwick I, and Callaghy T eds. 2001 *Right-Sizing the State: The Politics of Moving Borders* Oxford University Press, Oxford.
Walker R and Mendlovitz S eds. 1990 *Contending Sovereignties: Redefining Political Community* Lynne Reiner, Boulder, CO.

Of particular interest is the *Borderline* series of monographs published by the University of Minnesota Press, including:

Shapiro M and Alker H, eds. 1996 *Challenging Boundaries: Global Flows, Territorial Identities.*
Soguk N 1999 *States and Strangers: Refugees and Displacements of Statecraft.*

Political geography

Chisolm M and Smith D eds. 1990 *Shared Space: Divided Space: Essays on Conflict and Territorial Organization* Unwin Hyman, London.
Cox K 2002 *Political Geography: Territory, State and Society* Blackwell, Oxford.
Dikshit R 1997 *Developments in Political Geography: A Century of Progress* Sage, New Delhi.
Glassner M and Fahrer C 2004 *Political Geography* 3rd edn. John Wiley, New York.
Hooson D ed. 1994 *Geography and National Identity* Blackwell, Oxford.
Muir R 1997 *Political Geography: A New Introduction*. John Wiley, New York.
O'Laughlin J ed. 1994 *Dictionary of Geopolitics* Greenwood Press, Westport, CT.
Shelley J et al. 1996 *Political Geography of the United States* Guilford, New York.
Storey D 2001 *Territory: The Claiming of Space* Pearson Education, Harlow, UK.
Taylor P 1989 *Political Geography: World Economy, Nation-State, Locality* 2nd edn. Longman Scientific, London.

Topical Works

Economic globalization

Cox K ed. 1997 *Spaces of Globalization: Reasserting the Power of the Local* Guilford Press, New York.
Sassen S 1996 *Losing Control? Sovereignty in an Age of Globalization* Columbia University Press, New York.
Sassen S 1998 *Globalization and its Discontents: Essays on the New Mobility of People and Money* New Press, New York.

Indigenous peoples of North America

Biolsi T 2001 *Deadliest of Enemies: Law and the Making of Race Relations On and Off Rosebud Reservation* University of California Press, Berkeley.
Fixico D 1998 *The Invasion of Indian Country in the Twentieth Century* University Press of Colorado, Niwot, CO.
Fouberg E 2000 *Tribal Territory, Sovereignty, and Governance: A Study of the Cheyenne River and Lake Traverse Indian Reservations* Garland Press, New York.
Frantz F 1999 *Indian Reservations in the United States: Territory, Sovereignty, and Socioeconomic Change* University of Chicago Press, Chicago.
Harris C 2002 *Making Native Space: Colonialism, Resistance, and Reserves in British Columbia* University of British Columbia Press, Vancouver.
Sutton I ed. 1985 *Irredeemable America: The Indians' Estate and Land Claims* University of New Mexico Press, Albuquerque.

Privacy

McGrath J 2004 *Loving Big Brother: Performance, Privacy and Surveillance Space* Routledge, London.

McLean D 1995 *Privacy and its Invasion* Praeger, Westport, CT.

Parenti C 2003 *The Soft Cage: Surveillance in America: From Slavery to the War on Terror* Basic Books, New York.

Petronio S 2002 *Boundaries of Privacy: Dialectics of Disclosure* State University of New York Press, Albany, NY.

US–Mexico border

Andreas P 2000 *Border Games: Policing the U.S.–Mexico Divide.* Cornell University Press, Ithaca, NY.

Dunn T 1996 *The Militarization of the U.S.–Mexican Border 1978–1992: Low Intensity Conflict Doctrine Comes Home* Center for Mexican American Studies, Austin.

Martinez O 1994 *Border People: Life and Society in the U.S.–Mexico Borderlands.* University of Arizona Press, Tucson.

Nevins J 2002 *Operation Gatekeeper: The Rise of the "Illegal Alien" and the Making of the U.S.–Mexico Boundary* Routledge, New York.

Journals

While scholarly work on territoriality can be found in many academic journals, the following are more likely than most to yield useful results.

Alternatives
Annals of the Association of American Geographers
Antipode
Diaspora
Environment and Behavior
Environment and Planning D (Society and Space)
Geopolitics
Global Society
International Migration
International Migration Review
International Studies Review
Millennium
Political Geography
Refugees

The Internet

The internet has profoundly changed the ways in which information – and misinformation – is produced, put into circulation, and consumed. Because territoriality is as pervasive and significant as it is, it stands to reason that there are countless websites that pertain to the topic one way or another. To begin with, thousands of territorially defined governmental units large and small have a presence on the internet. Most, no doubt, do not directly implicate territoriality as an issue. But some may be useful for examining official policies concerning territory. For example, the website of the US Customs and Border Patrol – an agency of the Department of Homeland Security – contains a wealth of information about the practical workings of border work (**www.cbp.gov**). Particularly interesting are its "image libraries," such as "Border Patrol Image Library" and "Concealment Methods Image Library" accessible through the "America's Frontline Collection." Similarly, Australia's Department of Immigration and Multicultural and Indigenous Affairs maintains a website (**www.immi.gov.au**) that contains information about illegal immigration, border patrol, and detention facilities. The internet can also be used to access information about specific territorial disputes. For example, one might compare interpretations about Jammu and Kashmir presented by the Indian Ministry of External Affairs (**www.mea.jov.in**) with those offered by the Pakistani government (**www.infopak.gov.pk/public/kashmir/kashmir.htm**). Kurdistan is also the subject of a number of websites, such as **akakurdistan.com** and **krg.org**, the official website of the Kurdistani regional government in Iraq.

In addition to official (or quasi-official) sites there are also advocacy sites that challenge official policy. To use the same approaches as above, one might usefully compare Humane Borders (**www.humaneborders.org**), an organization dedicated to providing humanitarian assistance to people crossing the US–Mexico border ("we must take death out of the immigration equation") to Ranch Rescue (**www.ranchrescue.com**), which identifies Mexican migrants as "an Army of Scum" and asks, "Is there any question that every American needs to be armed to the teeth?"

Likewise, there are a number of organizations that are critical of Australia's policy toward refugees and asylum seekers (for example, Refugees Australia [**refugeesaustralia.org**], the Australian Refugee Association [**ausref.net**], and the Refugee Council of Australia [**refugeecouncil. org.au**]). Contending positions on any number of territorial issues can be found on the internet.

In a more scholarly vein there are a number of useful websites that are germane to the topic and which give access to a wide range of information. The Department of Geography's Centre for Border Research at the University of Nijmegen in the Netherlands maintains a website (**www.ru.nl/ncbr**) that includes access to the *Journal of Borderland Studies* and has other valuable links. Other academic sites include those maintained by the Border Research Studies Network (**www.crossborder.ifg.dk**), the Geopolitics and International Relations Research Centre at the University of London (**www.soas.ac.uk**), the University of Warwick's Centre for the Study of Globalization and Regionalization (**www2.warwick.ac.uk/fac/soc/csgr**), and the Centre for International Borders Research at Queen's University, Belfast (**www.qub.ac.uk/cibr**). The latter has especially useful links.

A third general type of internet resource that is worth mentioning for comparative purposes includes those sites that might best be described as alternative anti-territorial. These include sites promoting "infiltration," "urban exploration," or trespassing, such as **www.urban_exploration.com** (exploring "forbidden areas that few people see, and that is the thrill"), **www.infiltration.org** ("going places you're not supposed to go"), and **www.thederilectsensation.com** ("it's about breaking free of the maze"). These sites commonly have links to allied projects throughout the world. Also worth mentioning are sites dedicated to squatting such as **www.squat.freeserve.co.uk** and **www.squat.net** (compare **www.landlordzone.co.uk**). Other anti-territorial sites include **www.noborder.org**, **www.antimedia.net/xborder**, **www.borderwatch.net**, and **www.contrast.org**. Of course, given the nature of the internet and the relatively ephemeral nature of alternative sites, this listing may be of antiquarian interest by the time this book is published.

Bibliography

Acuña R 1996 *Anything but Mexican: A History of Chicanos* Harper & Row, New York.

Agnew J 1993 Representing Space: Space, Scale and Culture in Duncan J and Ley D eds. *Place/Culture/Representation* Routledge, London 251–271.

—— 1998 *Geopolitics: Re-Visioning World Politics* Routledge, London.

—— 1999 Mapping Political Power Beyond State Boundaries: Territory, Identity and Movement in World Politics *Millennium* 28, 499–521.

—— 2000 Commentary *Progress in Human Geography* 24, 91–93.

—— and Corbridge S 1995 *Mastering Space: Hegemony, Territory and International Political Economy* Routledge, London.

Aiken S et al. eds. 1998 *Making Worlds: Gender, Metaphor and Materiality* University of Arizona Press, Tucson.

Altman I 1975 *The Environment and Social Behavior: Privacy, Personal Space, Territory and Crowding* Brooks-Cole, Monterey, CA.

Alvarez R 1999 Toward an Anthropology of Borderlands: The Mexican–U.S. Border and the Crossing of the 21st Century in Rosler M and Wendl T eds. *Frontiers and Borderlands: Anthropological Perspectives* Peter Lang, Frankfurt am Main 225–238.

Amnesty International 2003 *Israel and the Occupied Territories. Surviving under Siege: The Impact of Movement Restrictions on the Right to Work* London.

Anderson E 2000 *The Middle East: Geography and Geopolitics* Routledge, London.

Anderson J and O'Dowd L 1999 Borders, Border Regions and Territoriality: Contradictory Meanings, Changing Significance *Regional Studies* 33, 593–604.

Appadurai A 1990 Disjuncture and Difference in the Global Cultural Economy *Public Culture* 2, 1–23.

—— 1996 Sovereignty Without Territoriality: Notes for a Postnational Geography in Yeager P ed. *The Geography of Identity* University of Michigan Press, Ann Arbor 40–58.

Archer C 2004 A Prison with your own Key all in the Name of Security! *Palestinian Monitor* March 21 (www.palestinemonitor.org).

Ardley R 1966 *The Territorial Imperative* Athenaeum, New York.

Ashley R 1987 The Geopolitics of Geopolitical Space: Toward a Critical Social Theory of International Politics *Alternatives* 12, 403–434.

—— 1988 Untying the Sovereign State: A Double Reading of the Anarchy Problematique *Millennium* 17, 227–262.

Barnard A 1992 Social and Spatial Boundary Maintenance among Southern African Hunter-Gatherers in Casimir M and Rao A eds. *Mobility and Territoriality: Social and Spatial Boundaries among Foragers, Fishers, Pastoralists and Peripatetics* Berg, Oxford 137–152.

Barth F 1969 *Ethnic Groups and Boundaries: The Social Organization of Cultural Difference* Little Brown, Boston.

Bartram D 1996 Foreign Workers in Israel: History and Theory *International Migration Review* 32, 303–326.

Bassin M 2003 Politics from Nature in Agnew J, Mitchell K, and Ó Tuathail G eds. *A Companion to Political Geography* Blackwell, Malden, MA 13–29.

Bauman Z 2004 *Wasted Lives: Modernity and its Outcasts* Blackwell, Malden, MA.

Benda-Beckmann F von 1979 *Property in Social Continuity: Continuity and Change in the Maintenance of Property Relationships through Time in Minangkabau, West Sumatra* Martinus Nijhoff, The Hague.

—— 1999 Multiple Legal Constructions of Socio-Economic Spaces: Resource Management and Conflict in the Central Moluccas in Rosler M and Wendl T eds. *Frontiers and Borderlands: Anthropological Perspectives* Peter Lang, Frankfurt am Main 131–158.

Berland J 1992 Territorial Activities among Peripatetic Peoples in Pakistan in Casimir M and Rao A eds. *Mobility and Territoriality: Social and Spatial Boundaries among Foragers, Fishers, Pastoralists and Peripatetics* Berg, Oxford 375–396.

Bickerton I and Klausner C 1995 *A Concise History of the Arab–Israeli Conflict* 2nd edn. Prentice-Hall, Englewood Cliffs.

Bornstein A 2002a Borders and the Utility of Violence: State Effects on the "Superexploitation" of West Bank Palestinians *Critique of Anthropology* 22, 201–220.

—— 2002b *Crossing the Green Line Between the West Bank and Israel* University of Pennsylvania Press, Philadelphia.

Brawley M 2003 *The Politics of Globalization: Gaining Perspectives, Assessing Consequences* Broadview, Peterborough, ON.

Bregman A *Israel's Wars: A History Since 1947* Routledge, London.

Brenner N 1999 Beyond State Centrism? Space, Territoriality, and Geographical Scale in Globalization Studies *Theory and Society* 28, 39–78.

Brown B 1987 Territoriality in Stokols D and Altman I eds. *Handbook of Environmental Psychology* John Wiley, New York 505–531.

Brown C 1992 *International Relations Theory: New Normative Approaches* Columbia University Press, New York.

B'Tselem 2002 Land Grab: Israel's Settlement Policy in the West Bank (www.btselem.org).

—— 2003a Attacks on Israeli Civilians (www.btselem.org).

—— 2003b Behind the Barrier: Human Rights Violations as a Result of Israel's Separation Barrier (www.btselem.org).

——2003c New Orders in Barrier Enclaves: 11,400 Palestinians Need Permits to Live in their Homes (www.btselem.org).

Buzan B 1996 The Timeless Wisdom of Realism in Smith S, Booth K, and Zalewski M eds. *International Relations Theory: Positivism and Beyond* Cambridge University Press, Cambridge 47–65.

Casimir M 1992 The Determinants of Rights to Pasture: Territorial Organization and Ecological Constraints in Casimir M and Rao A eds. *Mobility and Territoriality: Social and Spatial Boundaries among Foragers, Fishers, Pastoralists and Peripatetics* Berg, Oxford 153–204.

——and Rao A eds. 1992 *Mobility and Territoriality: Social and Spatial Boundaries among Foragers, Fishers, Pastoralists and Peripatetics* Berg, Oxford.

Clark I 1989 *The Hierarchy of State: Reform and Resistance in the International Order* Cambridge University Press, Cambridge.

Cohen A 1985 *The Symbolic Construction of Community* Ellis Horwood, Chichester.

Cohen S 1973 *Geography and Politics in a World Divided* Oxford University Press, New York.

——1994 Geopolitics in the New World Order: A New Perspective on an Old Discipline in Danko G and Wood W eds. *Reordering the World: Geopolitical Perspectives for the 21st Century* Westview, Boulder, CO 15–48.

Connolly W 1996 Tocqueville, Territory and Violence in Shapiro M and Alker H eds. *Challenging Boundaries: Global Flows, Territorial Identities* University of Minnesota Press, Minneapolis 141–164.

Cook J 2003 A Cage for Palestinians *International Herald Tribune* May 27.

Cusimano M ed. 2000 *Beyond Sovereignty* Bedford, Boston.

Dalby S and Ó Tuathail G 1996 The Critical Geopolitics Constellation: Problematizing Fusions of Geographical Knowledge and Power *Political Geography* 15, 451–456.

Darby P 2003 Reconfiguring "the International": Knowledge Machines, Boundaries, and Exclusions *Alternatives* 28, 141–166.

Davis U 1987 *Israel: Apartheid State* Zed, London.

De Genova N 1998 Race, Space and the Reinvention of Latin America in Mexican Chicago *Latin American Perspectives* 102, 87–116.

Decker S and Van Winkle B 1996 *Life in the Gang: Family Friends and Violence* Cambridge University Press, Cambridge.

Delaney D 1998 *Race, Place and the Law 1836–1948* University of Texas Press, Austin.

Deutsch J-G et al. eds. 2002 *African Modernities: Entangled Meanings in Current Debate* Heinemann, Portsmouth, NH.

Dieckhoff A 2003 *Invention of a Nation: Zionist Thought and the Making of Modern Israel* Columbia University Press, New York.

Dikshit R 1975 *The Political Geography of Federalism: An Inquiry into Origins and Stability* John Wiley, New York.

Dodds K and Atkinson D eds. 2000 *Geopolitical Traditions: A Century of Geopolitical Thought* Routledge, London.

Dodge T 2003 *Inventing Iraq* Columbia University Press, New York.

Domosh M and Seager J 2001 *Putting Women in Place: Feminist Geographers Make Sense of the World* Guilford, New York.

Donnan H and Wilson T 1999 *Borders: Frontiers of Identity, Nation and State* Berg, Oxford.

Doty R 2001 Desert Tracts: Statecraft in Remote Places *Alternatives* 26, 523–543.

Egan T 2004 Risky Dream and a Rising Toll in the Desert at the Mexican Border *New York Times* May 23.

Falah G 1996 The 1948 Israeli–Palestinian War and its Aftermath: The Transformation and De-signification of Palestine's Cultural Landscape *Annals of the Association of American Geographers* 86, 256–285.

—— 2003 Dynamics and Patterns of the Shrinking of Arab Lands in Palestine *Political Geography* 22, 179–209.

Farsoun S 1997 *Palestine and the Palestinians* Westview, Boulder, CO.

Finnie D 1992 *Shifting Lines in the Sand: Kuwait's Elusive Frontier with Iraq* Harvard University Press, Cambridge, MA.

Flynn D 1997 "We Are the Border": Identity, Exchange, and the State along the Bénin–Nigeria Border *American Ethnologist* 24, 311–330.

Forsberg T 1996 Beyond Sovereignty, Within Territoriality: Mapping the Space of Late-Modern (Geo)politics *Cooperation and Conflict* 31, 355–386.

Frazier D 1998 *The U.S. and Mexican War: 19th-Century Expansionism and Conflict* Macmillan, New York.

French L 2002 From Politics to Economics at the Thai–Cambodian Border: Plus ça change … *International Journal of Politics, Culture and Society* 15, 427–470.

George J 1994 *Discourses of Global Politics: A Critical (Re)introduction to International Relations* Lynne Reiner, Boulder, CO.

Giddens, A 1991 *Modernity and Self-Identity: Self and Society in the Late Modern Age* Blackwell, Cambridge.

Glazer D 2003 Zionism and Apartheid: A Moral Comparison *Ethnic and Racial Studies* 26, 403–421.

Glossop R 1993 *World Federalism? A Critical Analysis of Federal World Government* McFarland, Jefferson, NC.

Goffman E 1971 *Relations in Public: Microstudies of the Public Order* Basic Books, New York.

Gottmann J 1973 *The Significance of Territory* University of Virginia Press, Charlottesville, VA.

Greenwald E 2002 *Reconfiguring the Reservation: The Nez Perces, Jicarilla Apaches and the Dawes Act* University of New Mexico Press, Albuquerque.

Griggs N 2002 Atzlan and Amalgamation *The New American*, May 6, 16–21.

Grosby S 1995 Territoriality: The Transcendental, Primordial Feature of Modern Societies *Nations and Nationalism* 1, 143–162.

Gupta A and Ferguson J 1997a Beyond "Culture": Space, Identity and the Politics of Difference in Gupta A and Ferguson J eds. *Culture, Power, Place* Duke University Press, Durham, NC 33–51.

—— 1997b Discipline and Practice: The Field as Site, Method and Location in Anthropology in Gupta A and Ferguson J eds. *Anthropological Locations: Boundaries and Grounds of a Field Science* University of California Press, Berkeley.

Halper J 2000 Palestine: Dismantling the Matrix of Control *Peacework* February (www.afsc.org/pwork).

——2002 Bantustans and Bypass Roads: The Rebirth of Apartheid? *Global Dialogue* 4, 35–44.

Hanieh A 2003 Israel's Clampdown Masks System of Control *Middle East Report* February 14 (www.merip.org).

Hartshorne R 1950[1969] The Functional Approach in Political Geography reprinted in Kasperson R and Minghi J eds. *The Structure of Political Geography* Aldine, Chicago 34–49.

Harvey D 1985 The Geopolitics of Capitalism in Gregory D and Urry J eds. *Social Relations and Spatial Structures* St. Martins, New York 129–163.

——2000 *Spaces of Hope* University of California Press, Berkeley.

Hasenclever A et al. eds. 1997 *Theories of International Regimes* Cambridge University Press, Cambridge.

Haskell T 1977 *The Emergence of Professional Social Science* University of Illinois Press, Urbana.

Hass A 1999 *Drinking the Sea at Gaza: Days and Nights in a Land under Siege* Metropolitan Books, New York.

——2002 Israel's Closure Policy: An Ineffective Strategy of Containment and Repression *Journal of Palestine Studies* 31, 5–20.

Heffernan M 2000 Fin de Siècle, Fin du Monde? On the Origins of European Geopolitics in Dodds K and Atkinson D eds. 2000 *Geopolitical Traditions: A Century of Geopolitical Thought* Routledge, London 27–51.

Held D and McGrew A 2002 *Globalization/Anti-Globalization* Polity, Cambridge.

Herek G and Berrill K eds. 1992 *Hate Crimes: Confronting Violence against Lesbians and Gay Men* Sage, Newbury Park, CA.

Hiro D 2001 *Neighbors not Friends: Iraq and Iran after the Gulf Wars* Routledge, New York.

Home R 2003 An "Irreversible Conquest"? Colonial and Postcolonial Land Law in Israel/Palestine *Social and Legal Studies* 12, 291–310.

Hudson Y ed. 1999 *Globalism and the Obsolescence of the State* E. Mellen, Lewiston, NY.

Hussein H and McKay F 2003 *Access Denied: Palestinian Land Rights in Israel* Zed, London.

James P 1972 *All Possible Worlds: A History of Geographical Ideas* Odyssey, Indianapolis.

Kantor M 1998 *Homophobia: Description, Development, and Dynamics of Gay Bashing* Praeger, Westport, CT.

Kasperson R and Minghi J eds. 1969 *The Structure of Political Geography* Aldine, Chicago.

Kearney 1998 Transnationalism in California and Mexico at the End of Empire in Wilson T and Donnan H eds. *Border Identities* Cambridge University Press, Cambridge 117–142.

Kearns G 2003 Imperial Geopolitics in Agnew J, Mitchell K, and Ó Tuathail G eds. *A Companion to Political Geography* Blackwell, Malden, MA 173–186.

Kedar A 2001 The Legal Transformation of Ethnic Geography: Israeli Law and the Palestinian Landholder 1948–1967 *New York University Journal of International Law and Politics* 33, 923–1000.

—— 2003 On the Legal Geography of Ethnographic Settler States: Notes Towards a Research Agenda in Holder J and Harrison C eds. *Law and Geography* Oxford University Press, Oxford 401–444.

Khalidi R 1997 *Palestinian Identity: The Construction of Modern National Consciousness* Columbia University Press, New York.

Kimmerling B 1983 *Zionism and Territory: The Socio-Territorial Dimensions of Zionist Politics* Institute of International Studies, Berkeley.

—— 1989 Boundaries and Frontiers of the Israeli Control System: Analytical Conclusions in Kimmerling B ed. *The Israeli State and Society: Boundaries and Frontiers* State University of New York Press, Albany.

—— and Migdal J 2003 *The Palestinian People: A History* Harvard University Press, Cambridge, MA.

Klein J 1990 *Interdisciplinarity: History, Theory and Practice* Wayne State University Press, Detroit.

Krasner S 1983 *International Regimes* Cornell University Press, Ithaca.

—— 1999 *Sovereignty: Organized Hypocrisy* Princeton University Press, Princeton, NJ.

—— 2001 Rethinking the Sovereign State Model *Review of International Studies* 27, 17–42.

Lapid Y 2001 Identities, Borders, Orders: Nudging International Relations Theory in a New Direction in Albert M, Jacobson D and Lapid Y eds. *Identities, Borders, Orders: Rethinking International Relations Theory* University of Minnesota Press, Minneapolis 1–20.

Latham M 2000 *Modernization as Ideology: American Social Science and "Nation Building" in the Kennedy Era* University of North Carolina Press, Chapel Hill, NC.

Lefebvre H 1991 *The Production of Space* Blackwell, Oxford.

Levy G 2003 The Occupation's Latest Wrinkle is a Separation Fence and its Permanent Gates: A Visit at "Open Sesame" Time *Ha'aretz* August 8.

Ley D 1983 *A Social Geography of the City* Harper & Row, New York.

Little R 1996 The Growing Relevance of Pluralism in Smith S, Booth K and Zalewski M eds. *International Relations Theory: Positivism and Beyond* Cambridge University Press, Cambridge 66–86.

Livingstone D 1993 *The Geographical Tradition: Episodes in the History of a Contested Enterprise* Blackwell, Oxford.

Lukes S 1986 *Power* New York University Press, New York.

Lyman S and Scott M 1967 Territoriality: A Neglected Sociological Dimension *Social Problems* 12, 236–249.

Maghroori R 1982 Introduction to Major Debates in International Relations in Maghroori R and Ramberg B eds. *Globalism versus Realism: International Relations' Third Debate* Westview, Boulder, CO 9–22.

Mandaville P 1999 Territory and Translocality: Discrepant Idioms of Political Identity *Millennium* 28, 653–673.

Martinez R 2001 *Crossing Over: A Mexican Family on the Migrant Trail* Metropolitan Books, New York.

Mbembe A 2000 At the Edge of the World: Boundaries, Territoriality, and Sovereignty in Africa *Public Culture* 12, 259–284.

—— 2003 Necropolitics *Public Culture* 15, 11–40.

McDonnell J 1991 *The Dispossession of the American Indian 1887–1934* Indiana University Press, Bloomington.

McDowell L and Sharp J eds. 1997 *Space, Gender and Knowledge: Feminist Readings* Arnold, London.

Meehan M 1996 The By-pass Roads Destroy Hopes for Future Palestinian Autonomy *Washington Report on the Middle East* April 8–9.

Migra A 1992 Roma Territorial Behaviour and State Policy: The Case of the Socialist Countries of East Europe in Casimir M and Rao A eds. *Mobility and Territoriality: Social and Spatial Boundaries among Foragers, Fishers, Pastoralists and Peripatetics* Berg, Oxford 259–279.

Migration News 2001 INS: Border Deaths, Trafficking vol. 8, July.

Minghi, J 1963[1969] Boundary Studies in Political Geography reprinted in Kasperson R and Minghi J eds. *The Structure of Political Geography* Aldine, Chicago 140–159.

Moore S 1986 *Social Facts and Fabrications: "Customary Law" on Kilimanjaro 1880–1980* Cambridge University Press, Cambridge.

Morrill R 1981 *Political Redistricting and Geographical Theory* Association of American Geographers, Washington.

Newman D ed. 1985 *The Impact of Gush Emunim: Politics and Settlement in the West Bank* St. Martin's, New York.

—— 2002 The Geopolitics of Peacemaking in Israel-Palestine *Political Geography* 21, 629–646.

—— 2003 Boundaries in Agnew J, Mitchell K and Ó Tuathail G eds. *A Companion to Political Geography* Blackwell, Malden, MA 123–137.

Niemann M 2003 Migration and the Lived Spaces of Southern Africa *Alternatives* 28, 115–140.

Ó Tuathail G 1994 Displacing Geopolitics: Writing on the Maps of Global Politics *Society and Space* 12, 525–546.

—— 1996 *Critical Geopolitics* University of Minnesota Press, Minneapolis.

Ohmae K 1999 *The Borderless World: Power and Strategy in the Interlinked Economy* Harper, New York.

Ortiz V 2001 The Unbearable Ambiguity of the Border *Social Justice* 28, 96–112.

Paasi A 2000a Territorial Identities as Social Constructs *Hagar* 1, 91–113.

Paasi A 2000b Commentary *Progress in Human Geography* 24, 93–95.

—— 2003 Territory in Agnew J, Mitchell K and Ó Tuathail G eds. *A Companion to Political Geography* Blackwell, Malden, MA 109–122.

Padilla F 1992 *The Gang as an American Enterprise* Rutgers University Press, New Brunswick, NJ.

Palafox J 2000 Opening up Borderland Studies: A Review of U.S.–Mexico Militarization Discourse *Social Justice* 27, 56–72.

Pappe I 2004 *A History of Modern Palestine: One Land, Two Peoples* Cambridge University Press, Cambridge.

Parker G 1998 *Geopolitics: Past, Present and Future* Pinter, London.

Peretz D 1993 *Palestinian Refugees and the Middle East Peace Process* United States Institute of Peace Press, Washington.

Perry N 2003 Is It a Fence? Is It a Wall? No, It's a Separation Barrier. *Electronic Intifada* August 1 (www.electronicintifada.net).

Purdum T et al. 2003 *A Time of Our Choosing: America's War in Iraq* Times Books, New York.

Rabinowitz D 2001The Palestinian Citizens of Israel, the Concept of a Trapped Minority and the Discourse of Transnationalism in Anthropology *Ethnic and Racial Studies* 24, 64–85.

Rappaport M 2003 A Wall in their Heart *Yedioth Aharonoth* May 23.

Ratzel F 1896[1969] The Laws of the Spatial Growth of States in Kasperson R and Minghi J eds. *The Structure of Political Geography* Aldine, Chicago 17–28 (originally published in German).

Research Unit for Political Economy 2003 *Behind the Invasion of Iraq* Monthly Review Press, New York.

Reuveny R 2003 Fundamentalist Colonialism: The Geopolitics of Israeli–Palestinian Conflict *Political Geography* 22, 347–380.

Rösler M and Wendl T 1999 *Frontiers and Borderlands: Anthropological Perspectives* Peter Lang, Frankfurt am Main.

Ross D 1991 *The Origins of American Social Science* Cambridge University Press, Cambridge.

Routledge P 1996 Critical Geopolitics and Terrains of Resistance *Political Geography* 15, 509–531.

Royster J 1995 The Legacy of Allotment *University of Arizona Law Review* 27, 1–78.

Ruggie J 1993 Territoriality and Beyond: Problematizing Modernity in International Relations *International Organization* 47, 139–174.

Sack R 1986 *Human Territoriality: Its Theory and History* Cambridge, Cambridge University Press.

—— 1997 *Homo Geographicus: A Framework for Action, Awareness and Moral Concern* Johns Hopkins University Press, Baltimore.

—— 2003 *A Geographical Guide to the Real and the Good* Routledge, New York.

Said E 2001 Palestinians Under Siege in Carey R ed. *The New Intifada: Resisting Israel's Apartheid* Verso, London 27–44.

Sauer C 1927 Recent Developments in Cultural Geography in Hayes E ed. *Recent Developments in the Social Sciences* J A Lippincott, Philadelphia.

Schimato T and Webb J 2003 *Understanding Globalization* Sage, London.

Scholte J A 1996 Beyond the Buzzword: Towards a Critical Theory of Globalization in Kofman E and Youngs G eds. *Globalization: Theory and Practice* Pinter, London.

Segal R and Weizman E eds. 2003 *A Civilian Occupation: The Politics of Israeli Architecture* Verso, London.

Sibley, D 1995 *Geographies of Exclusion* Routledge, London.

Sifry M and Cerf C eds. 2003 *The Iraq War Reader: History, Documents and Opinions* Touchstone, New York.

Silltoe P 1999 Beating the Boundaries: Land Tenure and Identity in the Papua New Guinea Highlands *Journal of Anthropological Research* 55, 331–360.

Smith C 2001 Closure: The Daily Reality of Israel's Occupation *Middle East Report* August 27 (www.merip.org).

Smith S 1995 The Self-Images of a Discipline: A Genealogy of International Relations Theory in Booth K and Smith S eds. *International Relations Theory Today* Pennsylvania State University Press, University Park, PA 1–37.

Soguk N 1996 Transnational/Transborder Bodies: Resistance, Accommodation, and Exile in Refugee and Migration Movements on the U.S.–Mexico Border in Shapiro M and Alker H eds. *Challenging Boundaries: Global Flows, Territorial Identities* University of Minnesota Press, Minneapolis 285– 326.

—— and Whitehall G 1999 Wandering Grounds: Transversality, Identity, Territoriality and Movement *Millennium* 28, 675–698.

Soja E 1985 The Spatiality of Social Life: Towards a Transformative Retheorization in Gregory D and Urry J eds. *Social Relations and Spatial Structures* St. Martins, New York 91–27.

—— 1989 *Postmodern Geographies: The Reassertion of Space in Critical Social Theory* Verso, London.

Storper M and Scott A 1986 *Production, Work and Territory* Allen & Unwin, Boston.

—— and Walker R eds. 1989 *The Capitalist Imperative: Territory, Technology and Industrial Growth* Blackwell, Oxford.

Strathern A and Stewart P 1998 Shifting Places, Contested Spaces: Land and Identity Politics in the Pacific *Australian Journal of Anthropology* 9, 209–224.

Tamir-Tawil E 2003 To Start a City from Scratch: An Interview with Architect Thomas M. Leitersdorf in Segal R and Weizman E eds. *A Civilian Occupation: The Politics of Israeli Architecture* Verso, London 151–161.

Taylor C 1989 *Sources of the Self* Harvard University Press, Cambridge, MA.

Taylor P 1994 The State as Container: Territoriality in the Modern World-System *Progress in Human Geography* 18, 151–162.

—— 1995 Beyond Containers: Internationality, Interstateness, Interterritoriality *Progress in Human Geography* 19, 1–15.

Taylor R 1988 *Human Territorial Functioning* Cambridge University Press, Cambridge.

Tesche B 2003 *The Myth of 1648: Class, Geopolitics and the Making of International Relations* Verso, London.

Tocancipá-Falla J 2000–01 Civilization and the Politics of Territorial Boundaries in Columbia *Cambridge Anthropology* 22, 36–61.

Torpey J 2000 *The Invention of the Passport: Surveillance, Citizenship and the State* Cambridge University Press, Cambridge.

US Department of State 2004 USINFO.STATE.GOV/gi/archive/2004/May

Van Valkenburg S 1940 *Elements of Political Geography* Prentice-Hall, New York.

Walker R 1984 The Territorial State and the Theme of Gulliver *International Journal* 39, 529–552.

—— 1989 History and Structure of the Theory of International Relations *Millennium* 18, 163–183.

—— 1993 *Inside/Outside: International Relations as Political Theory* Cambridge University Press, Cambridge.

—— and Mendlovitz S eds. 1990 *Contending Sovereignties: Redefining Political Community* Lynne Reiner, Boulder, CO.

Weizman E 2002 The Politics of Verticality (www.opendemocracy.com/debates).

Wilson T and Donnan H eds. 1998 *Border Identities: Nation and State at International Frontiers* Cambridge University Press, Cambridge.

—— 1999 Nation, State and Identity at International Borders in Wilson T and Donnan H eds. *Border Identities: Nation and State at International Frontiers* Cambridge, Cambridge University Press, 1–30.

Yetman D and Búrquez A 1998 A Case Study in Ejido Privatization in Mexico *Journal of Anthropological Research* 54, 73–95.

Yiftachel O 1998 Democracy or Ethnocracy: Territory and Settler Politics in Israel/Palestine *Middle East Report* Summer 8–13.

—— 2000 "Ethnocracy" and its Discontents: Minorities, Protests, and the Israeli Polity *Critical Inquiry* 26, 725–756.

—— 2002a Territory as the Kernel of the Nation: Space, Time, and Nationalism in Israel/Palestine *Geopolitics* 7, 215–248.

—— 2002b the Shrinking Space of Citizenship: Ethnographic Politics in Israel *Middle East Report* Summer 38–45.

Index

abjection 100
Absentee Property Law, Israel 128
Agnew, John 37, 57–8
ambiguity 90
Amnesty International 136–7
anarchy 37, 53
anthropology 9, 43–6, 61–3, 64
anti-Semitism 41, 107
apartheid 11, 19
Appadurai, Arjun 63
Arab–Israeli War (1948) 114
Ashley, Richard 54–5

Balfour Declaration 111–12, 127
Barth, Fredrik 43
biological imperative 72
bodies 47, 46, 61, 66–7
border control 64
border theory 63–7
borderlands 65
Bornstein, Avram 133–4
Brenner, Neil 68–9
British Mandate, Israel/Palestine 111
bypass roads, Israel/Palestine 142

castle doctrine 8
Catholic Church 14, 85
checkpoints, Palestine 134, 136–8
children 75, 101
civil rights movement 17

closures, Israel/Palestine 138
colonialism 22, 36, 46, 74
critical geopolitics 56
culture theory 61–3, 67, 86
curtilage 7–8

desegregation 16
desire 89
de-territorialization 2, 15–16, 27, 56,
    63, 96, 118, 144
disciplinarity 50
discourse 54, 91–4, 108, 144

environmental psychology 9
everyday life 66, 105, 123, 138

fear 89, 99
federalism 39, 95
feminism 52, 58, 60–1, 86, 97
free territory 48
functionalism 18–20

Gaza 109, 116, 119, 134–5, 138, 139
gender 12, 61, 86, 99
geography, human 9, 38–43, 46, 56–61
    Marxist 59
    political 39, 42, 45, 56
geopolitics 17, 39, 53, 56, 60
global territorialism 68
globalization 63, 67–8, 86, 96

Goffman, Erving 48–9, 67, 89
Green Line, Israel/Palestine 114, 118, 132–4, 137

Hartshorne, Richard 41–2
Holocaust 114
home 6, 7, 47, 75, 101
homophobia 93
Human Territoriality 50, 70–101
humane borders 3

identity 12, 55, 92, 94–7, 118–19
    Palestinian 109, 130, 133, 135–6
ideology 18, 23, 88, 92, 98, 107, 109, 144
indigenous peoples 3, 22, 73–4
inside/outside 3, 5, 14, 31, 33, 36, 55, 64
international regimes 37
international relations 9, 17, 35–8, 43, 45, 46, 52–6, 60, 62, 67
    realist v. idealist 37, 53, 57, 97
interpretation 28–30
Intifada 123, 133
Iraq 1–3, 42
irrationality 89
Israel/Palestine 32, 102–45
    see also checkpoints; closures; Gaza; Green Line; Intifada; Occupied Territories; separation barrier; settlements; West Bank

Jewish National Fund 104, 109, 114, 128
Jim Crow 11, 15, 19
Judaization of territory, Israel/Palestine 104, 108, 124

Kedar, Alexandre 124–5, 127
Kimmerling, Baruch 108–10
knowledge 37, 92
Kuwait 2

land tenure 21, 45–6, 105
Lefebvre, Henri 59–60
legitimacy 17

Marxism 59, 76, 80, 97
masculinity 93
McKellar v. Mason 7–8
meaning 14, 17, 28–30, 91
Mexican–American War (1848) 3
Mexican–US borderlands 3, 4
Mexican workers in US 3
modernity 12, 20–3, 28, 48, 52, 71, 73, 74, 82–5, 87–91, 95
    see also post-modernity; pre-modernity
modernization 21

al-Naqbah 116
nationalism 10, 95
Newman, David 102–3, 139
nomads 43–5
North American Free Trade Area 33
North Atlantic Treaty Organization 33

Occupied Territories 114, 119–23, 132–44
open fields doctrine 5, 30
Oslo Accords 121–3, 136, 142
Ottoman Land Code (1858) 105, 125

Paasi, Anssi 70, 95
penetration 48
personal space 48
political economy 21, 81, 83–4
politics 71, 97–9
post-modernity 52, 58, 60, 71, 86, 87–91
post-structuralism 51
power 16–17, 19, 30, 33, 75, 137
pre-modernity 74
present absentees 129
primitivity 81–3, 87, 93
prison 75
privacy 6, 8, 22, 93
production of space 75
property 5–6, 18, 22, 30, 32, 74, 99, 108, 109–11, 124–30
    defense of 7–8
psychology 49–50
public/private 5, 32, 61
public territory 47

race and racism 12, 15, 18, 19, 22, 86, 93, 94, 96
    see also anti-Semitism
Ranch Rescue 3
rationality 89–90, 101
Ratzle, Friedrich 39–40, 57
refugees 60
    Palestinian 116–18, 135–6
resistance 98
re-territorialization 16, 68–9, 103, 111–16, 118, 123, 125, 126, 130, 145

Sack, Robert 50, 70–101, 103, 128
scale 61, 67, 70
science 21, 84
seam area 143
separation barrier 143–4
settlements, Israeli 139–42
sex 48
sexuality 93
sheath 46, 67, 81
Sibley, David 99–101
signs 14, 28–9
Six Day War (1967) 119
sovereignty 17, 21, 23, 32, 36–8, 53, 74, 90, 93, 99, 110, 111–16, 127–8, 142, 144

space 14, 59, 75
spatial ontology 37
stall 49
surveillance 64, 141–2

Taylor, Ralph 49–50
territorial trap 57–8
territorialization 10, 11, 15–16
Trans-Jordan 113
translocality 55–6
turf 46–7

U.S. v. Oliver 5, 30, 32

Van Valkenburg, Samuel 40–1
verticality 31–3
    politics of, Israel/Palestine 141–4
violence 98, 119
voting districts 16

Walker, Rob 43–4
Weber, Max 76, 80–1
West Bank 121, 132–44
workplace 75

Yiftachel, Oren 108

Zionism 107–11, 113, 124–6